This is the Good Thing

Also by Stuart Albright

Blessed Returns
Sidelines
Bull City
Creative Writing 101
A World Beyond Home

This is the Good Thing

Choosing a Life of Service over Self

Stuart Albright

MCKINNON PRESS
2704 Bexley Avenue
Durham, NC 27707
(919) 943-6501

Special discounts are available on this book. To inquire, please contact Stuart Albright at stuartalbright@gmail.com.

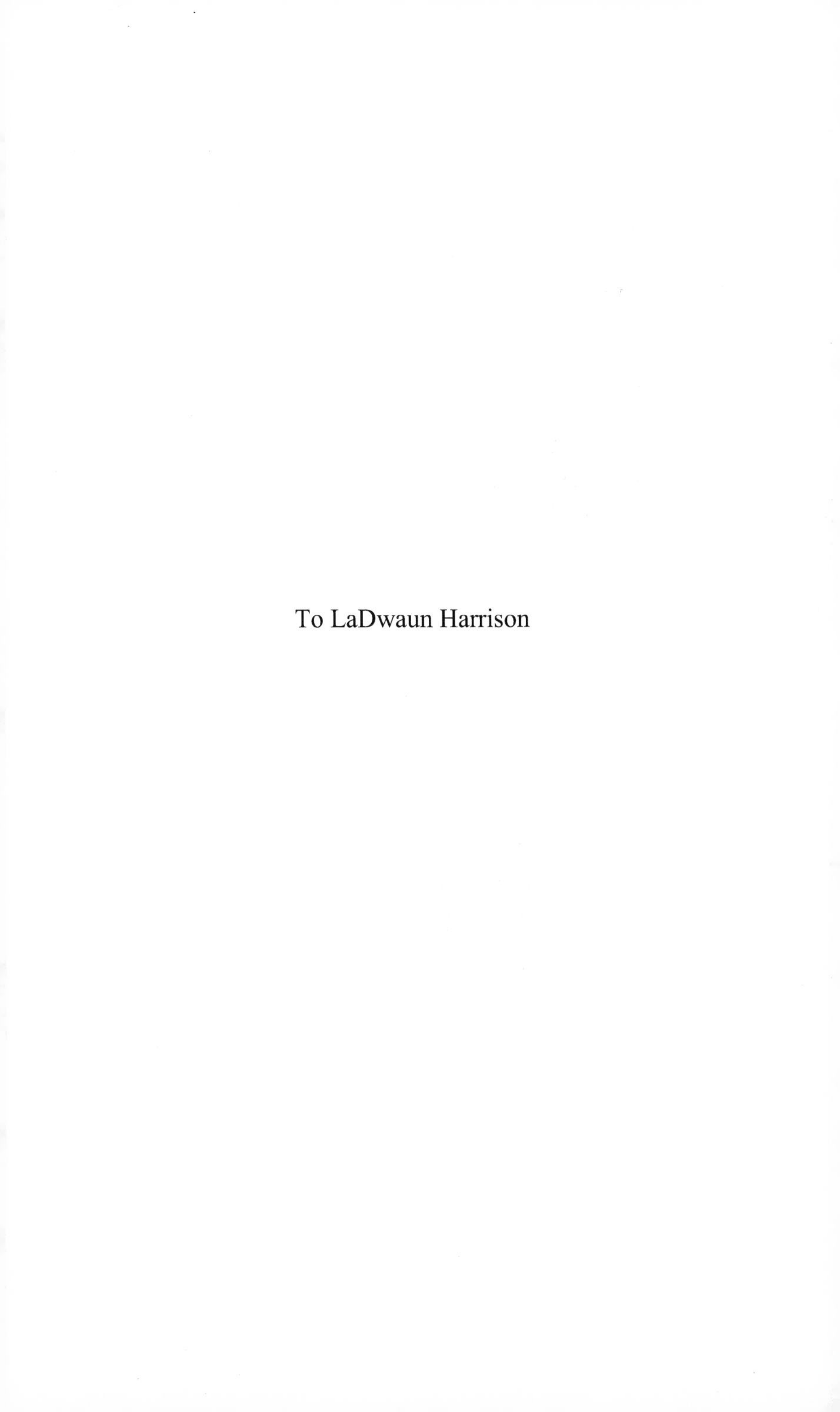

To LaDwaun Harrison

Prologue

Dear Brett and Cason,

This book is a letter for you. It's kind of a story too.

Ever since you were little, you've asked me to tell you a story each night before I tuck you into bed. For a while, every story had to be true. You wanted to learn about my childhood, or when you were just babies, or when your mom and I were newly married. You really loved stories about Uncle Rob, probably because he and I are two years apart, just like the two of you. I spent an entire summer telling you Uncle Rob stories.

Then there was the year when you wanted me to create my own stories for you. I'd place your stuffed animals on the edge of the bed, and they became the main characters in a complicated plot that I made up on the spot. Sometimes these stories were boring. Sometimes they were pretty interesting. You both loved the spontaneity of it, never knowing where these stories would lead us as your eyes grew wide with excitement and then slowly, slowly turned heavy with sleep.

I will never forget these moments with you – just talking, laughing, and being a family together. I hope these nighttime stories have made you feel loved. I hope they have made you feel special. I will always treasure our bedtime routine.

I treasure so many things about the two of you. So many moments where we have laughed together, talking well past your bedtime. You love to ask questions, and I've always tried to give you the right answers. I've tried to be a good father. For the longest time, I thought that to be a good father I had to say the right things. I had to pass on some of the wisdom I've learned over the years. These days I'm not so sure it works that way.

When you grow up, there is a chance that you will remember some of the things I've said. But more likely, you will remember *how* I said these things. You will remember the accumulated time we've spent together, night after night under the soft glow of the white lights strung around your door, the stuffed animals lined up against the wall, our laughter and our nightly prayers, followed by a kiss on each of your foreheads. You will remember the *feel* of our bedtime routine more than what we actually talked about. This will be your concept of home – the predictable rhythms of bedtime, 6:30 p.m., night after night. I look fondly on my own childhood because it had that sense of security. I knew that Mom and Dad were in control and they would never let anything happen to me. I knew what to expect. Everything was predictable. I hope that you feel the same way about these years. As you get older, the world will not always be so predictable. Difficult moments will rock the foundation upon which you stand. You will have to deal with sadness, grief, and fear. Yes, fear will come around in your weakest moments. But you don't have to be afraid. You are brave. You are strong.

Last week, all of us were stuck at home with the flu. I've never seen a sadder sight in our house, all four of us sniffling and coughing and fighting off 102-degree fevers. For the first time in 17 years of teaching, I called in sick. If this had happened a few years back, I would have been pretty stressed out. *What will the substitute teacher be like? Will my students behave while I'm gone?* These questions used to sum up my approach to work – it was my identity, my calling. Only *I* could teach these kids. How would they carry on without me? And it wasn't just school. I was supposed to coach Brett's basketball team on Saturday, then lead a meeting the following day. All of these things had to go on without me. And guess what, they *did* go on without me.

As I stayed home sick with the two of you and with your mom, I didn't think about school at all. Maybe it was the fact that I was shaking and feverish. Or maybe it was something else; perhaps I'd finally come to realize that in the big scope of things, I am merely a single human being. I am small and I am limited. I don't say this to put myself down; I love my work and my family, and I think that I contribute well to our community. But I am small. The world does not revolve around me. I used to think that it did, but it doesn't. As the two of you get older, I hope that you will understand this. All of us are small and the world is incredibly big. We have to do our part and understand that our part is only a small piece of a larger picture. That is enough.

When I went back to school this past Monday, Brett drew a colorful picture for me with a bunch of green hearts and the words, "Dear Dad. I love you. Take on the day." This is some of the best advice I have ever received, and I am so thankful for it.

Take on the day. Live every moment fully, knowing that while we are small, we can do big things as long as our hearts are in the right place.

So what is this book really about?

That's hard to say. Writing has always been a way for me to bring order to my disordered thoughts. I kept a journal in college to help me work through my fears and insecurities. I've continued this process into adulthood by writing a handful of books.

Writing gives me clarity. When I start a new book I often feel like I'm standing at the edge of a dense forest. I know there is a clearing on the other side, but I don't know the best way to get there. So I step into the forest and go down one wrong path after another, colliding with trees, losing my way in a fit of frustration and then starting over again. But I never stop looking for the right path.

Eventually, I always find a way out of the forest. It can be long and winding, but the path is always there.

At this point I'm still looking for the right path.

In this book I want to pass along a few things I've learned as an adult. The past twenty years of my life have been full of happiness and sadness, successes and mistakes, big sweeping moments and little details that have made me who I am today. There have been far too many times when I've felt unsettled, when it has been hard for me to find peace. For most of my adult life I've struggled with this feeling. The world tells us to keep striving onward, reaching for fame and fortune and all the trappings of success – all the stuff that is supposed to make us happy but only leaves us feeling empty inside.

When the two of you become adults, I hope that you will turn out better than me. That's really every parent's hope. I want you to love others and to shine a light in your own little corner of the world. I want you to be happy. I want you to make other people happy.

I'm not sure when you will read this. Right now you are nine and seven. These lessons probably won't make sense until you are much older.

I want you to know how much I love the two of you, how my world changed forever when you were born.

I've tried to be a good father, and I know that I've made mistakes. You will make mistakes too – this is unavoidable. But the measure of a man is the way he grows from his mistakes.

It takes courage to admit mistakes. It takes courage to be humble. The world will encourage you to puff out your chest and to sing louder than the people around you. The world will encourage you to let the desire for attention shape your values, always striving for the next big challenge and forgetting about the people closest to your heart.

You must avoid this.

Don't let the spotlight define your worth as a human being. Shine the spotlight onto someone else. Lift them up so that their beauty shines for the entire world to see. You may never get the credit, but that's not the point. That is *never* the point.

This may not make a whole lot of sense right now. But after you've read this book, I hope that some of it will. Please know that I am incredibly proud of you. Your mother and I love you with all of our hearts.

Part I
The Problem

The Seduction of the Self

What does it mean to live a good life? I've thought about this question a lot, particularly on days when my life seems to be transitioning from one season to the next. High school graduation marks the end of one of those seasons.

I am a high school teacher, and every year for the last 17 years I have sat on the floor of Duke's Cameron Indoor Stadium with the rest of the faculty and watched another group of seniors receive their diplomas. There's something beautiful and tedious about watching the same event for 17 years in a row. First the beauty: I feel rooted in this place, and I like the connections I've made with my co-workers, my students, and their families. Graduation is a sacred act because it is the culmination of 13 years of school. These students have overcome struggles and heartbreak, long nights filled with homework and stress about tests and parents going through divorces and remarrying and families shattered by addiction and neglect. They get to walk across a stage and know that they've accomplished something real. They've made it.

But these ceremonies can also be tedious. I can almost close my eyes and predict what will happen from the beginning of the ceremony to the end. North Carolina in the early summer is always incredibly humid. The girls stumble along in too-high heels. The boys adjust their crooked ties. I see tears and I hear laughter. We applaud as these seniors move their tassels from right to left with their parents cheering wildly, then the band plays "Pomp and Circumstance" on a continuous loop as the new graduates file out of the stadium and into the adult world.

Afterwards I weave through the crowd and hug the students I know, posing for pictures and telling everyone how very proud I am.

What I don't tell them is that I am also a little bit scared. In the coming years, some of these students are going to be happy. Some of them are going to struggle with depression. As teachers, we try to do everything we can to prepare them for the real world, but life can be a brutal teacher for all of us.

Over the years, I've witnessed what it's like for young people to wrestle with their futures. They're standing on the edge of adulthood, and they're still trying to decide who they want to become. Should they go to college or the military? Should they move in with their boyfriend or break up? Go to college in-state or move out-of-state? Take drugs or avoid drugs? New car loans or new student loans?

The possibilities seem endless.

Of course, when the possibilities seem endless, the simplest response is to do nothing at all. So many of my students (and, more broadly, so many people in our society) are content to stand in one place, allowing the shifting tides of our culture to dictate their every move.

I've always been fascinated by the gap between what kids want and what they actually do. Young people don't like to have their future dictated to them. They want to be respected as individuals. They want to be heard.

That's one side of the equation. But here's the other side: those same kids – the ones who demand to be heard – rarely question the cultural norms that actually dictate their behavior, pulling them down the same well-worn path as everyone else. And they don't even realize what's at stake.

So I sit here for yet another graduation ceremony, smiling and high-fiving kids who will no longer be kids after they receive their diplomas. One stage of life comes to an end while another one begins.

The next day I will go back to my classroom – room 413, the same four walls that I've occupied for the past 17 years – and I will pack up my things for the summer. The posters on my walls are starting to wilt a little bit. Some of the class pictures are fading, especially the ones from my first couple years of teaching. Those students are probably in their thirties now. Before long I will teach their own children and this cycle will continue on and on until my body gives out and I finally turn out the lights for good.

In 1997, the psychologist Arthur Aron created an experiment to understand the ways in which people connect. He placed a series of strangers in a room together for 45 minutes and gave them a list of 36 questions to ask each other. The questions started out easy enough ("Would you like to be famous? In what way?") But they quickly went deeper and required each participant to be vulnerable ("When did you last cry in front of another person?") Dr. Aron found that when the right questions are asked, people open up to each other and connect in ways that rarely happen in our society today. Many of the participants became good friends. A year after the study, two of them got married and invited the whole lab to their wedding.

In 2015, a professor named Mandy Len Catron tried out the 36 question test with a colleague from work. They ultimately fell in love, and Catron's *New York Times* essay on the experience went viral.

"I wondered what would come of our interaction," Catron writes. "If nothing else, I thought it would make a good story. But I see now that the story isn't about us; it's about what it means to bother to know someone, which is really a story about what it means to be known."

Mandy Len Catron wanted to be known. My students want to be heard. All of us want someone to look us in the eyes when we speak and to see us for who we really are. We want to be loved in spite of our imperfections, our weaknesses, and our vulnerabilities.

But the world pushes us to act differently. How many of us are willing to put our imperfections on the table and say, "Here, this is me. This is who I am. Take it or leave it." How many of us are willing to look directly at someone and truly see them? Arthur Aron's study is famous for its 36 questions, but one part of the study gets far less attention. At the end of the session, each of the participants was asked to stare directly at their partner for four straight minutes. Just the thought of doing this makes me nervous. But it's a powerful idea: when do we ever give someone our total, undivided attention, even for ten seconds, let alone four minutes? We rarely take the time to truly *know* someone else.

Life isn't as simple as it used to be.

I hate this sentiment, partly because it's true (but not in the ways that we care to acknowledge), and partly because it makes me sound old and out of touch. Life wasn't always better in the past. If I had the choice to go back to any previous stage of my life and to live it over again, I would stay right where I am at age 40 with a wife and two kids. I wouldn't change any of my mistakes, or anything I've learned in the past. Every stage of my life has been more fulfilling than the one before it.

Yes, life is more complicated these days. Technology connects millions of people. It has lifted generations of families out of poverty and created advances that have saved lives. But technology is a beautiful thing until it's not. I see this in the glazed-over way that my students look at their phones. In the way that *I* look at my phone, feeling it in my pocket and knowing that I am only a swipe away from discovering something, anything, limited only by the speed of my fingertips. The world tells us that this access to information is a good thing. Sometimes it is. Sometimes it's not.

Take social media, for example. In theory, we should embrace any platform that connects people more effectively. The internet has made the whole world feel smaller. People are less isolated than ever before, and our rapid technological advancements are, on the whole, good for capitalism.

Social media is a tool for communication and a tool for self-promotion, but it is also a time suck that provides limited value to a small group of people.

The writer Seth Godin makes this point better than I can: "The Mona Lisa has a huge social media presence. Her picture is everywhere. But she doesn't tweet. She's big on social media because she's an icon, but she's not an icon because she's big on social media."

If everyone is special, shouldn't we see social media as a way to magnify our "specialness" to the world? For some people, this works. For the rest of us, these platforms occupy too much space in our brains.

I see the damage that the social internet has done to young people. Twitter, Snapchat, and Instagram have created communities online, but they have also paved the way for a more poisonous trend: the seduction of self-promotion.

Our brains get a dopamine rush every time we post something online. We get affirmation that we exist, that we matter. But this affirmation quickly fades away. Like any addictive drug, we have to go back for another hit, a slightly bigger jolt of affirmation to equal the previous high. At this point we're hooked on an artificial feeling that is almost completely insulated from the real world.

Most of the time our online persona is an airbrushed version of our real selves, filtered and devoid of the real flaws that make us human – and, ironically, more desirable to others.

Teenagers live much of their lives in this carefully curated world. They document everything noteworthy, although most of what they highlight is designed to draw out a constant feedback loop of affirmation.

I dream of a world in which young people reject this way of thinking. It *is* possible, because young people like to be on the cutting edge of what is new and trendy. Perhaps one day the boldest and most rebellious among them will decide to delete their social media accounts and lead a new trend: young people occupying public spaces in large groups, socializing face to face with no filters and no likes and no trending topics. Just *being* together, face to face.

When I was in high school the popular fashion trend was to buy all of your clothes at Goodwill. This was a style in and of itself – you wanted to look like you didn't care about your clothes. Before long, everybody was uniquely clothed in the same kinds of baggy jeans and threadbare t-shirts.

Kids want to be different, as long as it's the right kind of different.

I've always been fascinated by the contradictory behaviors of teenagers. They want to be brave and to make a name for themselves, but they usually wait for someone else to step forward first. They pay attention to every new trend so that they can act accordingly, but they rarely have the vision and the creativity to boldly step out on their own.

Sometimes they do step out on their own. It's incredibly inspiring to watch a young person take a risk. I live for these moments as a teacher. And if I could do one thing in my classroom to alter the universe in some significant way, I would figure out how to spread this boldness to others. What if that was our mission as a society? What if we learned how to harness the creative spark in all of our students, our neighbors, and our co-workers? What if each of us decided to elevate that spark in just one person?

The world would be a very different place.

It wouldn't be filled with a million filtered images and trending topics, that's for sure.

The culture of self-promotion is not limited to teenagers. It extends all the way to the highest reaches of our government.

In his inaugural speech, President Donald Trump spoke of America as a troubled land filled with carnage. "I am your voice," Trump said. "Only I can fix it."

We are partly to blame for this. We expect our leaders to be larger-than-life saviors. Only they can save us, while we sit back passively and complain about our broken electoral system and the leaders that have been entrusted to rescue us.

The world of politics and the world of entertainment continue to move closer together into one toxic mix. Reality TV celebrities and twitter provocateurs capture our attention by constantly drawing attention to themselves. Even bad publicity is good publicity, as long as the clicks keep coming and the names keep trending. And we eat it up. We refuse to look away, to imagine a different path.

I believe in the inherent worth of all people. But I don't believe that we should turn people into idols. We waste so much of our lives following the mundane activities of celebrities, living through them and ignoring the rich details of our own experiences. We live vicariously through others because it is easier that way, letting the world happen around us while we absorb everything passively. We lose so many opportunities to connect with our neighbors, our co-workers, and our very selves.

The Seduction of the Self invades every part of our national culture.

I'm a huge sports fan, but I can't watch pro football or pro basketball anymore. Multi-million dollar contracts have made a lot of athletes ridiculously wealthy, but they have also warped the dreams of countless young men.

If you take money out of the equation, sports have tremendous value. They teach life lessons such as hard work, selflessness, resilience in the face of defeat. But so many of the football players I have coached in high school – and their parents – see sports as their only path to wealth and prominence. Forget college. Forget life lessons. This is about getting paid. And everyone in their orbit wants a piece of the pie.

A few years ago I coached a guy named Devin. He was a talented wide receiver who eventually played for an elite college program in the Atlantic Coast Conference. If there was ever a player who had the skillset to make it to the NFL, it was Devin. He was smart and fast, and he had a natural gift for football that simply can't be taught.

Devin was also incredibly unlucky. While he managed to become an All-American in college, he also broke the same bone in his foot three times. Then his collarbone. His pro dreams were steadily fading, but he refused to let them die.

College football allowed Devin to graduate with a bachelor's degree in sociology and a master's degree in kinesiology, fully paid for. His life seemed set. He had plenty of options.

Around this time, Devin started to date an attractive girl at a nearby college. I met her a couple of times when they came home to visit, and she seemed nice enough. She just looked like someone who was used to getting her way. Devin happily obliged.

After graduating from college, Devin signed a free agent contract with the Philadelphia Eagles. He worked hard and made the first round of cuts. Then the second round of cuts. He and his girlfriend even caused a viral sensation after their elaborate pre-game handshake was caught on video. When a reporter interviewed Devin's girlfriend, she said that the attention was good for her modeling career.

Eventually, the final pre-season game arrived. Devin played well, catching a couple of long passes and looking every bit like he belonged in the NFL. His chances of making the 55-man roster looked promising.

But the next day he was cut.

Devin's whole life had been building up to this moment. Pro football was his dream, his destiny ever since he was running circles around the other seven-year-olds in Pop Warner. What would he do now?

That same day, Devin's girlfriend dumped him.

"I need to live a certain lifestyle," she told Devin. "And you can't provide that for me anymore."

About a month later, Devin came by my classroom for another visit. He was alone this time, his ego decidedly in check.

"Can I teach your class today?" Devin asked me.

For the next thirty minutes, Devin lectured my English class on the importance of hard work and humility in everything you do. He was eloquent and grounded in a way that I had never seen from him before. He looked happier too.

Of course, he had to make a little dig about his ex-girlfriend at the end.

"Women these days," he said to my class, shaking his head. "Women don't know what loyalty means anymore."

For extra emphasis, he wrote the word "loyalty" on the board in big looping letters. Followed by a frowny face.

My students laughed as Devin shook his head slowly, as if he was trying to dislodge the memory from his brain forever.

Fame is a powerful drug, and it works its spell on young people in subtle ways.

We are taught from a young age to follow our passions. But how do we even know what to be passionate about? For most kids, almost every hour of the day is accounted for. You get up, eat breakfast, spend all day at school, then divide your evenings between extra-curriculars and homework. If you're lucky, you will learn something in school that peaks your interest. Or perhaps your sport or your after-school club will instill some kind of lesson that nudges you in the direction of a life-long profession. That's the hope, at least.

Kids are constantly looking for role models to tell them how to behave. Sports heroes have a tremendous pull on their attention. So do actors, musicians, and YouTube stars. Now we can add Instagram "influencers" to this list. An influencer is anyone with a large social media following. They dominate the world of fashion and travel, and many of them are famous for simply being famous. They rarely create something new and fresh, like the best artists, but they know how to craft a public persona. Companies are willing to spend millions of dollars to get these influencers, who are often no older than 18, to endorse their product. Young people pay close attention to this, and they begin to think that fame and fortune can be theirs if they emulate these social media stars. They just have to tap into the zeitgeist the way these influencers do – wear the right clothes, look the right way, say the right things to boost their list of followers. It's all about creating a brand. Forget talent. Forget working hard. It's about crafting an image for other people to follow.

It starts small. You post a picture and a witty comment and feel the rush of attention from your followers. What if you don't get enough likes? Push the envelope further. Stir up some controversy. Maybe say something you don't really believe just to drive the "conversation." See if that works. Take better selfies, make sure the light shines just right to accentuate your best features. Post more content. Maintain your daily streaks. Keep striving, always staying plugged in no matter what time of day it is. Fame is just on the horizon, and with it all the money and attention you need to live a happy and carefree life.

Of course, life rarely works out that way. And where does that leave us? Usually disappointed, doubtful, and devalued. Too often, we fold into ourselves and stay there, afraid to venture into the world and share what we have to offer.

In the acclaimed documentary *They Will Not Grow Old*, director Peter Jackson set out to bring World War I to life in a fresh new way. Jackson sorted through countless hours of 100-year-old black and white footage. In these old film reels, silent soldiers lurch forward in rapid speed due to the hand-cranked cameras of that long ago era. Using the same computer technology that made his *Lord of the Rings* movies so popular, Jackson slowed the footage down, added warm and natural colors, and then brought in actors and a sound crew to bring the footage completely to life. The final product is stunning and incredibly life-like. That's the whole point: this *was* real life. These were real 18-year-old kids fighting and dying for their country, sleeping in the mud and suffering from wounds that would never fully heal. When I watch a movie like this, I gain a newfound appreciation for everything that these soldiers went through. I see them for the first time.

We need to see people more often for who they really are. Peter Jackson used computer technology. In my classroom I use writing. Many of my students are undocumented immigrants. They write beautifully about their experiences in America, about their hopes and fears, the loneliness that comes from being stuck in a roach-infested apartment and never leaving for fear of an ICE raid, the cold of the desert at night in places like the Rio Grande Valley, carrying gallon water jugs and walking for hours on end, all for the chance at a better life. My students may write about these things in broken English, but the beauty is clearly there. Like Peter Jackson with his CGI technology, I look beneath the typos and grammar errors. The story comes to life for me, and when my immigrant students revise their writing and present it to their classmates, these stories come to life for everyone, bright and shining as the morning sun.

It can be hard for us to see someone for who they really are. I've been guilty of this in the past, and I'm still guilty of it. But I try to remind myself that most of the people we come in contact with have a rich interior life that we simply don't understand. That's not to say that we can't understand them; we just haven't taken the time to ask the right questions, to see them for who they are and who they can become.

Growing up, I was uncomfortable around gay people. More to the point, I was uncomfortable *about* gay people. I didn't actually know anyone who was openly gay. When I went to graduate school, my supervisor was a lesbian. She invited me over to her house, where I met her partner of over twenty years. We ate a good meal together, played with their golden retriever puppy, laughed and told stories about our families. I felt completely at ease around them. Of course I felt completely at ease – these were kind people living their lives just as I was. They just happened to have a different sexual identity from me. Most of the time, this is all it takes for our long-held biases to come crashing down: a simple meal with someone who is different from us. A face to face conversation. We have to be willing to lean into the initial discomfort, though.

Empathy requires us to see the complexity in other people. Instead, we'd rather focus on the complexity within ourselves. We obsess over it, smoothing out the rough edges and covering up the flaws. Then we broadcast the good stuff for everyone to see. Let them be jealous. Let them give us a little dose of praise. Let them believe that we have everything figured out when we really don't.

Why am I bothered so much by the Seduction of the Self? I think it's because I see myself reflected in so many of these issues. I am a flawed human being. I can be selfish. I tend to live inside my head way too much. I can empathize with these seductions because I have experienced all of them at some point in my life.

I should start there.

I can't move forward until I understand where I have been. I always encourage my students to be vulnerable, to admit when they are wrong and to own up to their flaws. Maybe I should practice what I preach. Let's start with my own story and move out from there.

My Story
(And How I Got Things Wrong)

I was painfully shy as a child. I hated to go to birthday parties because I couldn't bear to leave my mom behind. I cried on my first day of kindergarten for the same reason.

School dances were the worst form of torture for me. I had no sense of rhythm, and I knew that if someone saw me dancing they would immediately start to laugh, making everyone around me laugh, especially the pretty girl I was dancing with – the one who was a head taller than me with smooth, cool hands compared to my sweaty palms, my bird chest stuck beneath an oversized coat and a clip-on tie, my cheap leather shoes moving awkwardly to the smooth saxophone solos of Kenny G, multi-colored strobe lights accentuating the early 90s hairstyles all around me.

Yes, hell is a middle school dance. I break into a cold sweat just thinking about it.

For most of my childhood, I obsessed over the way people thought about me. I liked girls but never had the guts to ask them out. What would they say? Would they laugh in my face, or worse, would they simply ignore me? What I wouldn't give to be able to read a girl's mind, to know where she stood without having to risk rejection. It would make my life so much easier.

Instead, I kept quiet. Looking back, I wasn't all that different from most kids. The future is uncertain, and your mind creates all the worst possible scenarios: I'll never be good enough, handsome enough, wealthy enough, popular enough. Sometimes I wonder if children are drawn to fantasy novels because their brains are so used to creating unrealistic scenarios that rarely fit into the actual world. Children can't project their future selves because they have no way of seeing life as it is and as it will be in the future. If every day is a mystery waiting to unfold, the world can feel like a really scary place. At least it was a scary place for me.

So I became quiet. My thoughts ran in circles and did cartwheels, but I kept everything inside. On the outside, I just looked serious and sad most of the time.

I remember long car rides with my dad, sitting next to him in the passenger seat. I'm staring out the window into nothing. My headphones are on, and I'm listening to some sad song on my portable CD player. Probably something moody and slow, lots of somber piano and horns (but definitely *not* Kenny G.) I'm thinking without really thinking, just folding into myself and watching the world spin around me. I am a passenger in this car and a passenger in this fast-paced world, taking in the sights and sounds and reflecting them back on my own life, wondering where I fit in, where I don't fit in, who I am, who I will become. I feel completely alone even though I am surrounded by love.

I'm not sad, really. I just feel overwhelmed by it all. The world seems so big and so uncertain. I want something, but I can't put my finger on what that thing is. A purpose, maybe? The assurance that I belong to something? To someone?

I think about all the lost time I spent on those car rides. My dad never pushed me to open up, although I'm sure that he would have loved to talk to me. I guess he knew what was going on. He knew that I'd grow out of it, or at least he hoped that I would grow out of it.

There will probably come a day when my own sons will treat me like this. For now, they never let my wife and I have an uninterrupted conversation. Their enthusiasm is boundless. They have questions about everything, staring wide-eyed at the world in all of its complexity. To them the world is full of wonder and beauty, and each new day is a chance to experience something for the first time. I'll keep answering their questions for as long as they ask them.

When I was their age, the world seemed to be full of possibilities. Then it started to shrink. I covered my ears with headphones. I no longer stared at the horizon. I folded into myself and waited for my life to happen.

I stayed that way for a really long time.

Things started to change in high school. I joined a football team, and for the first time I began to feel like I was part of something bigger than myself. I had this brand new family that was big and boisterous and very different from me. And they liked me. More than that, they *needed* me. I was one of eleven soldiers on the field. If I screwed up, the whole team suffered. We lost the battle. But when we won, the spotlight shined equally on all of us. We celebrated together, our voices so much louder in one collective shout than they ever could have been on their own. Sure, some of my teammates were more talented than the others. But each of us had a role to play. I found a way to fit in without sacrificing my identity. I could be myself. I could like the things that I liked. I could even laugh at my own flaws. All of this was okay as long as I carried my own weight. I had to contribute to the team, and once I did, I was like a seed planted in fertile ground, bearing more fruit than I ever could have expected on my own.

For the first time in years, I started to unfold. I walked down the hallways with my head held high, a smile on my face. I liked who I was. I could overcome any obstacle, accomplish anything I set my mind to.

I even fell in love with a girl.

Okay, falling in love kind of rocked my world. As a teenager there are two phases of adolescence: life before love and life after love. And I was in the thick of it. This girl was pretty and smart and, miracle upon miracles, she actually liked me too.

As a teacher, I always get a little scared when one of my students tells me that they've fallen in love. My mind immediately goes to the high school version of Stu Albright.

He is a kind and considerate boyfriend, but he will do anything for this girl. Luckily, she has a good head on her shoulders. She likes him back, but she isn't so in love with him that they travel down the serious path that young lovers sometimes do – fantasizing about their adult lives together after high school, a home, some kids, two lives intertwined.

Instead, they enjoy each other's company and try to figure things out along the way. Neither one of them has been in a serious relationship before, so there's a lot to think about. And then there's schoolwork. Football for Stu. A million college applications for her. High school Stu only applies to one school, his dream school. What kind of an idiot only applies to one school? He probably does this because his mind is in the clouds 99% of the time thinking about this girl.

Luckily, he gets into the college of his dreams.

Not long after that, the girl breaks up with him. He is devastated. He cries. He tries to win her back. He folds back into himself and obsesses over all of their good times together, wondering what went wrong.

As it turns out, the girl was not the best fit for high school Stu. I'm glad he got to know her. I'm glad he got to experience the kind of pain that feels overwhelming in the moment but strengthens you in the long run.

After high school I fell in love again. Three more times, actually. And each time I learned something. First off, I was drawn to very intelligent women. Their beauty expanded in front of me as I grew closer to each of them. This is a good thing, obviously, because surface-level beauty is fleeting and subjective. Any mature relationship has to go deeper. So looking back, I can say with confidence that I was moving in the right direction.

But I still had a long way to go. In addition to being attracted to intelligence, I also enjoyed feeling like a hero to some of my girlfriends. Two of them came from broken homes, and they appreciated my stability. I was willing to overlook the lingering effects of depression and family resentment, their anger towards organized religion, their erratic and reckless behavior. I was loyal to a fault, even when two of them cheated on me. *It wasn't her fault*, I kept telling myself.

Looking back, I can't believe I put up with so much. But I loved these girls, flawed as they were. I didn't know any better. Aside from my parents' own happy marriage, what was a successful partnership supposed to look like?

I stumbled into my twenties wondering who I wanted to be and what I wanted in a life partner. I was trying on skin after skin, hoping that one of them would fit. Each time I fell in love, I fell *hard*. The rest of the world simply stopped. I looked inward and stayed inward, oblivious to so many other things. I wasted so much time thinking about myself.

"The world doesn't revolve around you," my mom liked to say to me.

This used to drive me crazy when I was a kid, probably because it was so true. Now I find myself saying the same thing to my own sons. And to celebrities on TV, and to self-absorbed sports stars, and to members of Congress.

So many people absorbed by the Seduction of the Self.

As I became an adult, I felt the weight of my decisions pressing harder upon me. The real world was quickly approaching, but nobody had a script for me to follow. I had to learn from my own mistakes.

As I look back on my history with love, I see how lucky I am today. There I was in high school, fumbling along with a girl who just wasn't the right fit for me. I couldn't recognize it until she finally forced me to.

I wandered through the hallways of Ashbrook High School in a daze. The people around me might as well have been invisible. I never got to know their own complex stories, their struggles to grow and to love with open hearts. Perhaps all of us were wandering through those teenage years like tiny planets revolving in our own orbits. Sometimes we would intersect, but usually we wouldn't. Life is like that sometimes. We come across someone new and decide, in a fleeting moment, whether to make them a part of our story. We have no way of knowing whether they will play a small part or a central role. All we can see is a happy ending or a sad ending, or perhaps no ending at all. This is scary, but this is how it was always meant to be.

And so I wandered down the hallways with my head in the clouds or down at my feet, but never straight ahead. If my eyes were truly open, I would have seen my future wife walking nearby. I was too blind or too dumb to see it at the time. She was right there, always smiling, always kind to everyone she met. Even to Stu Albright, who was stumbling along as the world rotated in circles around him.

I did nothing to deserve her. I just got lucky.

Growing up is like that sometimes. We fall in love with one person and never realize that the right match is just a few steps away.

We need to open our eyes and take the blinders off. And once we can finally see, we need to step out of the forest and help someone else to find the clearing on the other side. And when we do, we'll find our own path. It will be brightly lit, clear as day.

Let's flash forward a few years. I made it through college with my dignity pretty much intact. Then graduate school. In the spring of 2002 I was lucky enough to get a good teaching job in Durham, North Carolina. I was becoming a stable adult, paying rent and health insurance and all the stuff that adults are supposed to do. My life consisted of a lot less drama than high school. This was a good thing because who wants to live like a teenager, drifting along the highs and lows of adolescence? Not me.

But I do have some vivid memories from that time in my life.

Fall has always been my favorite season. The air gets crisp and the excitement of a new school year blends into the predictability of a set routine. Life takes on a definite shape.

It was about 9:00 a.m. on a Friday, and I was teaching one of my most difficult classes – repeat freshmen. Some of the kids were pushing 20 years old. A few had spent a significant amount of time behind bars. Many of them were reading at about a third grade level.

These weren't bad kids. I actually enjoyed working with most of them, but when you teach a class full of third-year freshmen it's like lighting a match in an oil field – sure, everything will probably turn out okay, but there's always a chance for an explosion.

So I wasn't exactly pleased when an assistant principal pulled me out of class to supervise an assembly.

"What about my kids?" I asked.

"We'll bring in a sub."

I rolled my eyes. "You sure that's a good idea?"

I could hear the noise level ratchet up in my room as I walked down the hallway, grumbling to myself.

I kept on grumbling as I entered the auditorium, which was filled with 11th and 12th graders.

"What's this about?" I asked a teacher to my left.

"Surprise assembly," she responded. "The state superintendent is here."

I rolled my eyes again and crouched in the middle of the aisle, still trying to figure out why I needed to be here. I pictured my desk getting overturned right about now. Maybe a fight was breaking out between the gangbanger and the girl who just got back from a suspension for hiding a box cutter under her tongue.

I was barely paying attention as the superintendent finished her speech and another woman took to the stage. Apparently she was from the Milken Foundation.

"Good morning, students," the woman began. "Every year we travel around the country, honoring the best teachers in America."

There was scattered applause from the students, but mostly they continued talking amongst themselves.

The award, the woman continued, was kind of like the Oscars of teaching. "Today, I'm here to present the award to one of your own."

The crowd perked up at this.

All I could think about was my students throwing desks in my classroom while an overwhelmed substitute teacher cowered in the corner.

The auditorium got even more electric as the speaker mentioned the financial prize associated with the award.

Hmmm, I thought, I could do a lot with that kind of money. As a 5th year teacher, I was getting along fine, but my wife and

I weren't exactly breaking the bank. We still had student loans, a steep mortgage, plenty of bills to pay…

"The winner of this year's Milken Award for Excellence in Teaching goes to…"

There was a dramatic pause. The room got silent. For the first time I noticed the TV cameras in the back of the room.

"…Stuart Albright!"

Before I knew what was going on, I was lifted off of the ground and pushed forward to the stage. The auditorium erupted in applause. I'd taught many of these kids, and they were chanting my name over and over again. Cameras started clicking away. My wife Jenni suddenly appeared from behind the curtain.

Finally, I reached the front of the auditorium, and all I could see was a room full of bright lights and stomping feet. My legs felt like they were about to collapse. I felt overwhelmed, gratified, and embarrassed, all at the same time.

Above all, I felt unworthy.

Receiving the Milken Award was an incredible honor. To this day I am forever grateful for it.

The previous year I'd won Teacher of the Year for our district. A year after the Milken Award, I published a book about high school football that was featured on the front page of the *Raleigh News and Observer*.

I came to believe that this was the natural trajectory of my profession. You work hard, you impact the lives of other people, and you get recognized for your efforts.

I'm not foolish enough to think that I deserved any of this attention. Even after all these years, I still don't know what

I'm doing half the time as a teacher. I keep failing to reach kids, and I still beat myself up over these missed opportunities. I screw up again and again and again.

But back then, everyone thought I was a star. "Are you planning to leave teaching now?" several people asked me, as if being a good teacher wasn't enough. Who would stay after an award like this? I should take the money and run to greener pastures.

"Of course not," I always replied.

Why would I want to leave a job that makes me happy? I got to help people every day, innovate in my classroom, build a community the way I wanted to. And best of all, I got recognized for my efforts.

So I kept at it. Year after year after year.

I've collected the newspaper clippings from that Friday assembly in a binder. Sometimes I take out one of the articles and glance at it. There I am, wide-eyed with shock, looking goofy as always, albeit ten years younger with no gray hairs on my head.

Who is this guy? He's not me. Well, he *is* me, but we're two different people now.

These days, the newspaper article is turning yellow with age. I'm a much better teacher now, still imperfect, but better still. I do my job well, but I no longer expect anything special in return. I don't ask my students for affirmation. And I sure as hell don't expect to win any more cash prizes for a job well done.

I'm old enough to know that I was lucky back then. A few people noticed something in me that they admired, and they decided to make a big deal about it. I didn't deserve the attention. I don't deserve it now, even though I probably help a lot more kids these days than ever before. I don't know what's worse – that I liked the attention so much, or that I came to expect it.

Young adults – the so-called Millennial Generation – are under the microscope these days. Plenty of scholars have written about their lack of maturity, or resilience, or grit. And institutions are very much to blame for this shift. *Psychology Today* points out that more than 94% of college students are graduating with honors. "Safer to lower the bar than raise the discomfort level," the article states. "Grade inflation is the institutional response to parental anxiety about school demands on children." Researchers at Florida State University argue that "students are increasingly ambitious, but also increasingly unrealistic in their expectations," creating what they call "ambition inflation." This whole mentality starts early on, according to the *New York Times*, with national soccer foundations spending as much as 12% of their yearly budgets on trophies.

I've been particularly fascinated by a related trend: young professionals demanding a pat on the back for even the most basic achievements.

Was I really all that different in my early 20s?

I liked to have the spotlight on me. I worked hard, and I expected to be honored for my hard work. I saw the world in a carefully organized system of achievements and rewards. You do X, and you get Y in return. Public affirmation was the natural order of things.

But did it really make me happy? Not particularly. I relied on other people to keep me engaged as a teacher. It was all about me. Sure, I enjoyed working with my students, but this joy was always qualified by what I expected to get in return.

This doesn't mean that affirmation is necessarily a bad thing. In fact, one of the true marks of any healthy relationship is the give and take between both parties. Nobody wants to be around someone who is a constant burden to their friends and co-workers. Nobody is attracted to selfishness.

But my priorities were still off. My work was never just about *the work*. I needed people to tell me that I mattered. I needed a spotlight, a trophy, a hand-written card with a gift certificate inside.

All of these affirmations are nice, but they don't lead to long-term happiness.

Here's what real happiness looks like:

That morning in the auditorium, I hugged my wife and I thanked her for supporting me. I thanked her for sacrificing her time and energy so that I could put in long hours at work, knowing that I wasn't earning half of what our college friends were making as lawyers, doctors, and engineers.

It was a private moment between the two of us – nothing mind-blowing or particularly cinematic about it, just two people acknowledging that they have been through a lot together and are better off because of it.

Then the bell rang, and we both headed back to work.

After school, I got on the bus for our football game that evening. A bunch of my players hugged me and shook my hand. Then they went back to preparing for the game. We were playing our county rivals. Everybody was excited.

I fired up the bus and started to think about our game plan as I pulled out of the parking lot. The trees were just beginning to turn yellow and orange. The weather was cooling off. Thanksgiving and the football playoffs would be here soon.

By the time we arrived at the stadium, I had almost forgotten about the award ceremony. I was locked in to the present, surrounded by a bunch of players and coaches who meant so much to me. I was part of something bigger than myself.

Looking back, if I had to choose between that morning assembly with the lights shining down upon me, or that evening with the lights shining down upon all of us, I would choose the Friday night lights every time.

My life had a pleasant rhythm with every season. Summers were always hot and time-consuming with football practices. The new school year began with excitement as we played our first game and all of that summer work became worth it. I got to know my new students, forming a dysfunctional family of sorts, the kind of bonding that happens when a group of people meet in a room day after day and start to trust each other. The same thing happened year after year, as predictable as the cool weather of autumn.

At the time, I was happy to be an assistant football coach. No matter how bad my day was at school, I could always step into the fresh afternoon air and experience something different. I could coach a group of teenagers who wanted to be there. I could laugh a little and jump around screaming after every big catch or bone-crushing hit. I coached the wide receivers and got to build lasting relationships with a dozen or so young men each year. We spent hours together in the heat of the summer, watching film, dissecting plays on the white board of my classroom. And football was just one part of my job; I did SAT prep with my players, as well as tutoring in English and study skills. To me, coaching involved the whole athlete – mind, body and soul. I loved every part of it.

Over time, my responsibilities increased. I became the JV head coach, and instead of working with a dozen players, I was responsible for all 50 of them. After school, my classroom overflowed with rambunctious freshmen and sophomores for study hall and film sessions – usually run by me alone, since the other coaches on staff were volunteers and couldn't get to practice until later in the afternoon.

Being a head coach was exhausting. But over time, I grew to like being in charge. Football is a complex game, and it attracts a diverse range of personalities. I liked the juggling act. I liked the challenge of creating order out of chaos. I liked feeling needed.

If you want a clear-cut validation of your worth, sports will provide that. All you have to do is win. Winning means that you are doing a good job. Losing means that you are a failure.

Obviously, this posed a problem over time.

We won a lot of football games, and every time we'd win, I told myself that I was a good coach. So did the parents of my players. Everybody was happy. Everything went smoothly.

But every game has a winner and a loser. And if you coach long enough, you are bound to lose some games.

Things began to change about five years ago.

One loss became two. Two losses became three. Bad luck reared its ugly head, and injuries began to pile up. I was working harder than I ever had before, but we kept on losing. I began to doubt myself.

So did the people around me. The parents of my players – the same ones who thought I could do no wrong when we were winning – made a bad situation even worse. They hurled insults from the stands, sent nasty emails to me (and to my principal and the superintendent) after particularly hard games. They threatened to send their kids to another school with better coaches who knew how to win and who could get their kids the "exposure" they needed for college scouts.

The negativity began to infect my players too. Some quit the team. Others turned on each other, starting fights or stealing cell phones and other valuables from the locker room.

Was I next? Would they start to turn on me too?

When we were winning, I loved the spotlight of being a head coach. But things were different now.

This is what it felt like:

I'm standing on the stage of a high school auditorium. The lights are on me, bright and harsh and showing every one of my flaws. A large audience is out there beyond the lights. I can't see them, but I can tell they are angry. They curse at me and throw things at the stage – rotten food, cups filled with blood – and I have to stand there and absorb every bit of it. I can't even cover my face for protection.

Another group of people are huddled at the edge of the stage, just out of reach of the objects being thrown my way. Some are hiding behind the curtain, waiting to see how this will play out. I recognize most of them: players, coaches, people I have come to rely on. They aren't happy to see me in this predicament, but they aren't doing anything to help me either.

And so I stand there under the lights, alone.

Powerless.

Around this time, I experienced a very different kind of powerless when my first son Brett came into the world.

I knew that parenting was going to be hard. Everybody told me so. But it's one thing to intellectualize this kind of change; experiencing parenthood is a totally different story.

I am an introvert in an extroverted job. When I get home, I like my downtime. I like to decompress, to read or to take a long jog. With the exception of my wife, I'd prefer to be by myself. I like to organize my life into controlled units of time. Life is crazy enough already, so I try to control the way I spend my free time. I like my evening routine because I can tailor it to my own needs. I don't have to rely on anybody else. I can be in control.

And then Brett was born. This helpless little boy with brownish green eyes, a scrunched-up face like an old man, and delicate little hands that would curl around my finger. Watching him sleep, my chest would tighten with a joy I had never felt before. He was so tiny and so fragile.

I'd listen to his breathing in the darkness of his bedroom as I rocked him to sleep. He looked so peaceful and serene, wrapped in a light blue blanket stitched with a little football around his initials.

My future wide receiver.

I'd sigh deeply and head next door to my own bedroom.

Twenty minutes later, a primal scream echoed throughout the house. Jenni went in to feed Brett and I tried to go back to sleep.

An hour later, another ear-splitting scream.

This time I stumbled out of bed and tried to calm Brett down. His eyes were wide open for another hour before I finally rocked him back to sleep, placed him oh-so-delicately in his crib, then made it across the room before the screaming started up again.

More rocking, more screaming.

I became delirious. Was it nighttime? Was it almost morning? Who was I at this point? A living, breathing person? A zombie? Some kind of half human, half baby rocking vessel that floated aimlessly through the night like a thick fog? I didn't know anymore.

When the CIA wants to extract information from an enemy combatant, I can imagine no better technique than sleep-deprivation. In those first harrowing nights of Brett's life, I would have given anything for an extra hour of sleep. Literally anything. I was no longer myself.

And that was probably a good thing.

Brett is nine years old now, and he loves to hear these stories about when he was a baby, when the sound of his crying could cut his mother and me down to a pile of tired bones.

Those first couple of months were extremely difficult. And when Cason was born two years later, the chaos multiplied exponentially.

But I can't imagine my life without them. I barely remember who I was before they were born. What did I do with all of that extra time? Why did I feel like I *needed* that extra time, like it was something that was owed to me, something necessary for me to function in the world? Why did I sell myself short for so many years?

I think the simple answer is that I didn't know any better. And when we don't know any better, we listen to the voices that tell us to look inward, to fold into ourselves, to take care of our own wants and needs first. Survival of the fittest.

But what does it mean to be "fit"? My wife and I get much less sleep these days. Our budget is tighter than ever before. We rarely get to have an uninterrupted conversation. But I am incredibly happy. Parenthood has rewired my brain. And like so much of this book, I hope that I am better because of it.

So I think I know what the problem is.

The problem is me. It's the focus on me, the attention to me, me, me – the tedious repetition of this phrase again and again in this chapter and in my life.

I'm tired of me. I want to move outside of myself and to think about other people. I want to understand the ramifications of this kind of shift, not only in my own life but in the lives of others. So many people are hurting, lonely, angry, self-centered, and empty. Yes, empty kind of sums it up.

How do we add joy to our lives in a way that is lasting and real? What does this look like, and how do we sustain it? I wish someone had talked to me about this when I was younger. Maybe it wouldn't have made a difference, but maybe it would have saved me a lot of wasted years.

Life is incredibly precious. The days feel long when we are in the midst of them, especially those tedious moments behind a desk at work or when we're paying bills at the kitchen table. We get sick. Loved ones die. Life doesn't turn out the way we want it to.

There were moments in my early years of parenting when life seemed to crawl by with an endless cycle of dirty diapers and the same monotonous routines. And then my boys were no longer babies anymore; they grew up before my eyes.

Older parents tell me it all happens in a flash. I'm starting to see that now. And it's not just parenting; life moves slowly and then speeds up in an instant. How will we live in the midst of so much uncertainty? What will we remember, and *how* will we be remembered when our days have come to an end?

I don't have many answers – but I think that's okay. Asking questions is the hardest part because it forces us to be honest with ourselves. We have to decide who we are and who we want to be. If we're not honest with ourselves, we let the world shape us instead of shaping our own destiny.

I want to be part of the solution instead of the problem. How about you?

Part II
The Shift

Why is this shift so hard?

Self-help books have a certain allure. They present a problem that we can relate to – something that we fear or that gnaws at our insecurities – and they give us a simple solution:

Try this diet and you will lose 15 pounds in a month, guaranteed!

Here are the five basic steps to a stress-free life!

Take this supplement twice a day and you will never get sick again!

I'm not sure how to market this book. Is it part of the self-help genre? Perhaps.

I'm challenging you, the reader, to think about your "self" – the way you fold inward or outward based on a number of factors both within and beyond your control. Yes, I'm offering advice. I want you to avoid the mistakes that I have made. I want you to live into the best version of yourself. I want you to help yourself.

I guess that makes this a self-help book.

But I have always believed in the power of nuance. In my classroom, some of the most teachable moments have come in the gray areas between certainty and anarchy. Teenagers don't like this place. They want answers. They may say that they want to think on their own, but our educational system doesn't always do a great job of training them to do this kind of uncomfortable work.

Adults are no different. The older we get, the easier it is to slip into a comfortable way of thinking. We watch Fox News or MSNBC. We're either pro-choice or pro-life, pro-immigration or anti-immigration, pro-guns or anti-guns. Gray areas make us uncomfortable. And in a struggling economy where our basic livelihoods are constantly under duress, who wants to add one more area of uncertainty? Believe me, I get it.

But I still believe in a better way.

We have to acknowledge the gray areas in our lives. We have to own them and embrace them with open arms, knowing that whatever conclusions we make will be hard-fought and uncomfortable but, ultimately, more lasting in the long run.

So here's the message of this book in a neat little package: we have to put other people first in order to have a fulfilling life and to create a better world for everyone.

Now let me unravel this package with a cold, hard truth: serving others is never simple. We have to start here because if we don't, the gray areas will consume us and make us give up the fight. We have to acknowledge that any real change involves pain and discomfort.

We all want to live a Hollywood ending. The foundation of storytelling feeds into this desire: a character wants something, and she has to overcome a series of obstacles to get what she wants. At the end of the story, we get a victory accompanied by soaring music and a dose of good feelings, but this high typically wears off as soon as we leave the movie theater.

I'm not saying we need to be suspicious of happiness. Far from it. I want happiness to be lasting. I want to experience happiness deep in my bones, to let it settle there as a shield for when the sadness comes back. And it will always come back. This is life, and life is full of discomfort and challenges.

I love to explore the Blue Ridge Mountains of North Carolina. These mountains are old and timeless, dotted with the pink buds of mountain laurels and the haze of low-hanging clouds. Sometimes I like to drive to the top of a mountain, which saves time and effort and still gives me the benefit of a pretty view. But I always prefer to reach a summit by foot. This takes longer, with the added benefit of muscle aches and blistered feet. But when I hike to the top of a mountain, the view feels different. The climb does something to my soul. The air feels fresher. The colors are more vibrant. I am present in a way that isn't possible without effort and struggle.

To serve others, we often need to embrace the "analog" or physical structures of the real world: the steep climb of a mountain hike, the dirt and sweat of a practice field, the grime under our fingers after a long day of manual labor. All of these things are tangible evidence of an active life. The effort matters. The struggle matters. In almost every part of our lives, we need something to push against.

We also need to be careful about *what* we push against.

So many of the great minds in American literature lived unhappy lives. Edgar Allen Poe died poor, drunk, and unrecognized. Same with F. Scott Fitzgerald. Zora Neale Hurston's gravestone went unmarked for several decades. Ernest Hemingway committed suicide.

Hemingway's death is particularly tragic. I love the famous line from his novel *A Farewell to Arms*: "The world breaks everyone and afterward many are strong at the broken places." Hemingway knew the world and he understood his place within it. Life is hard. Life is tragic. Our bodies are designed to absorb stress and, if the balance is just right, we can grow stronger from this stress. Hemingway's words had the power to transform millions of people, but in the end, they could not save him from his own depression.

Naturally, my students want to know if misery is a prerequisite for creativity.

No, I tell them. Fitzgerald did his best work when he was completely sober. Hurston wrote *Their Eyes Were Watching God* in a dizzying seven weeks while she was living within a vibrant Haitian community. Hemingway struggled to keep his four marriages intact, but his best work came when he was filled with love for another human being. The best writers, and more broadly the most successful innovators, achieve great things when they are able to balance the give and take between suffering and belonging.

It's good to have a wall in front of us, but it's helpful to be able to see what lies on the other side of this wall.

Like all of us, my life has been filled with ups and downs. I remember the high moments, but these memories are usually covered in a glossy afterglow. My low moments, on the other hand, are seared into my brain like a brand. These are the moments that define who I am. And they continue to define who I am, because life never moves in a straight line.

***

On a Friday in early November of 2015, I wrote a resignation letter.

For the first time in 14 years, I was no longer a football coach at Jordan High School.

At the end of the school day I submitted my letter to the front office. I walked down the hallway and nodded to coworkers and students as they headed home for the weekend, filled with laughter and boundless energy. It was a crisp fall afternoon with clear blue skies and the leaves turning a vibrant orange and red.

I put on a fake smile as I picked up the pace, trying not to show how I was really feeling.

How *was* I feeling?

Exhausted, for starters. And angry too. I was tired of the constant battle with parents who thought I was never good enough. I was tired of the pressure bearing down on my shoulders, the steady hum of voices telling me to do more, try harder, sacrifice more of myself than was humanly possible.

My stomach turned in knots as I carried these feelings inside, smiling at the people around me because I didn't want to draw attention to myself.

Eventually I walked upstairs to Coach Harrison's classroom, where our team was waiting to hear the news. A press release had been sent out that morning, so most of the kids already knew what was coming: after four years, LaDwaun Harrison was no longer the head varsity football coach at our school.

That didn't make the meeting any easier. I'd worked side by side with Coach Harrison for the past 14 years, and he has become one of my closest friends. We've bonded over a love for football and a passion for helping kids. LaDwaun is the kind of guy who can connect with just about anybody. He grew up in inner-city Durham, but he went to college at Wake Forest, so he can easily connect with people from all walks of life. We've spent thousands of hours together, trying to make a difference in the lives of young people. It never mattered that LaDwaun was black and I was white, or that I came to this city as an outsider while he was a Durhamite born and bred. I trusted him and he trusted me. We've been through a lot together, experiencing plenty of wins and plenty of heartbreaking losses, watching each other's children grow up, sharing our deepest hopes and dreams, working side by side in the dirt and the heat, cleaning musty locker rooms and folding thousands of football uniforms.

LaDwaun is also a really humble guy. He was a high school football legend at Hillside High School, but I never learned that from him. I had to dig up old press clippings and talk to his old teammates. This past year I taught his daughter, Tylah, in my creative writing class. She acts the same way as her dad, never drawing attention to herself even though she has a perfect GPA and will likely get in to every college she applies to. There's something special about watching a friendship grow over many years. I can still see Tylah stumbling around the locker room as a toddler while her dad and I fold uniforms, and then in a lightning-fast moment she is a 17-year-old student in my classroom, the female version of her father, filled with his best qualities and showing me that humility extends beyond time and across blood-lines.

But on this particular afternoon, humility felt more like shame.

Coach Harrison stood up to speak. Like me, he looked tired. Defeated. But as the head varsity coach, things were coming to an end in a much more public way for him.

LaDwaun handled the meeting with typical grace. His message was short and to the point: We simply didn't win enough games.

Then it was my turn to talk. My voice faltered as I said that I, too, was resigning. This was more of a surprise to them, judging from the sudden silence in the room. It hurt to see so many players staring back at me, guys that I've come to love as a JV head football coach and varsity assistant.

Before long the meeting was over. I hugged these young men and wished them well as I held back the tears. LaDwaun and I would still see them around school (we both planned to remain on the teaching staff at Jordan, at least for the time being), but the bond we had with these guys would never be the same.

As I drove home that Friday afternoon, my mind drifted back to the last 14 years … painting the game field in the dark, washing muddy uniforms at 11 p.m. after a JV football game, the hot summer practices, the night I coached a JV game while my wife went into labor (I was so consumed by the virtues of my job that I couldn't put my family first even then.)

And then I thought back to the previous summer, when I first started to realize that things were coming to an end. I spent the weekend with my family at the beach, where we stayed in a beautiful, ocean-front home. Brett and Cason played happily in the sand all day. Jenni and I enjoyed some precious time with her extended family.

But when Sunday came around, I headed back home by myself. We had football practice in the morning.

I gave up a whole week of vacation with my family because I was committed to these young men. I'd done this kind of thing for years, and looking back I'm amazed that Jenni put up with my absences for so long. For some reason it was different this time. I pulled up to my dark, quiet house that Sunday evening and thought about my boys playing happily on the beach with my wife. I placed my bag on the floor and let the silence of the living room sink in. Then I lost it. The weight of everything finally came crashing down around me. None of this was worth it anymore. But that didn't make it any easier. I was coaching football for all the right reasons. I'd found something in my professional life that was deeply worthwhile. I was helping people. I was serving others. This was a good, good thing. So why did I feel so empty?

A few weeks later, after our second straight loss to start the football season, I stood in the middle of Brett's birthday party, completely exhausted from coaching. I am ashamed to write these words. My oldest son was turning five and all I could think about was our next game. *How are we going to turn things around?* We lit the birthday candles. *What can we do differently?* We sang "Happy Birthday" as my family blurred to the background. *We've got to work harder. It's the only way out of this hole.*

Winning was the only solution. It would get the parents off our backs. Our players would stop bickering with each other. Maybe then I could feel like I was doing my job well.

But deep down I knew that winning wasn't enough.

Everything was turned upside down. Everything was going in the wrong direction.

Yes, you can have the best of intentions. Yes, you can commit yourself to a cause that is worthy and just. But it can still consume you. You can lose yourself in this cause, forgetting why you wanted to serve others in the first place. Life happens to you instead of the other way around. Before you know it, years have gone by, and when you finally look back on the blurred memories, it is often difficult to separate the good from the bad. You wake up as if from a dream, and you're left standing at your son's birthday party with your body present while your mind is far, far away.

I thought about all the moments that led up to that Friday afternoon resignation. I thought about the countless nights I came home after Brett and Cason were already asleep, watching their little chests rise and fall and feeling an incredible love for these two boys, regretting the lost time that I would never get back.

And for what?

I tried not to be angry. I tried to remember why I started coaching in the first place.

You see a whole lot of good when you coach for 14 years. You see troubled boys who turn into professors, engineers, and dependable fathers to their own children. You see how football can shape them into men of character, even during those losing seasons – especially during those losing seasons, because that's when someone's true character really comes to the surface.

Our football team wasn't very good that year. I won't deny it. The season was challenging for many reasons: we had a freshman quarterback and four sophomore linemen; one of our players broke his neck in a late season game; we dealt with injury after injury as the season progressed. For yet another year, LaDwaun and I were the only coaches in the building, working overtime to monitor study halls and keep our players out of trouble while still teaching a full class load. In the 14 years I had been at Jordan, not a single full-time faculty member was hired to coach football. It's hard enough to get good people to go into teaching. But throw in an additional 40 hours a week of coaching? Very few people are willing to make that kind of sacrifice.

As the losses piled up, so did the jeers from the stands, to the point where I didn't want my wife and sons to come to our games. The whole atmosphere was completely toxic.

But life is like that sometimes. Maybe I was a bad coach. Maybe it wasn't enough to care about something with all of your being, to sacrifice so much for a greater cause.

If nothing else, coaching has taught me humility.

When I got home that Friday afternoon, my son Brett was the first person to greet me. He didn't care whether I was a good coach or not. He just wanted to spend some time with his dad.

So that's what we did.

We got in the car and drove. I smiled as he told me about his day at school. Brett is a natural storyteller, and I love the way his voice picks up speed as he talks. I smiled as I listened to his story.

Just as the sun began to set, we reached Pilot Mountain in central North Carolina, which rises like a dome over the flat, rural countryside. I drove to the top of the mountain, and Brett bounded out of the car. The wind was sharp and cold with the rise in elevation. Brett pulled me by the hand to an overlook, and we gazed at the beautiful leaves down below, glowing brighter with the setting sun. We were the only people up here to witness this. Such an incredible view, always there but so often ignored by humans as we go about life, striving and worrying and changing with the seasons.

I hugged Brett and kissed him on the top of his head.

My headache was gone. The knot was loosening in my stomach. I still felt angry, but how could I focus on this anger when there was so much goodness around me?

When Brett gets older, he probably won't remember this night. After all, he was only five. Cason was only three, so he was too young to join us on the trip. Plus, he always hated to ride in a car when the sun went down. He used to wail like the world was coming to an end.

I have to write these memories down because I, too, will forget them. That's only natural, I guess, but I don't want to forget that day in November. I don't want to forget the knot in my stomach and the sadness of that team meeting. I don't want to forget the way that both of my boys smiled at me when I got home, hugging me and making me feel human again. Bringing me back to life.

I resigned from coaching in November. The movie version of my life would end on the top of Pilot Mountain with Brett and that beautiful setting sun.

But in the real world, I still had to go to work every day.

"Hey Coach, when are you leaving?" some of my students asked me. "I heard you got fired."

"Not from teaching," I told them. "Just from coaching."

"I signed up for your creative writing class next year," a girl asked me one day. "But since you won't be here, I had to change my schedule."

She turned and walked away before I could come up with an answer.

Other teachers thought I was leaving too. I started to wonder if my principal *had* fired me and somehow informed everyone in the school first. Needless to say, I didn't feel wanted here anymore.

Within a week, two schools in a neighboring district offered me a job, completely unsolicited.

Okay, this was getting a little weird. I guess I *should* start looking for work elsewhere. Football was a huge part of my job, but it wasn't my only identity, right?

During my planning period, I would sometimes sit under a tree next to my classroom and think about what I was going to do next. The tree had a lot of good shade and a nice wooden bench. The landscape around the tree looked like something out of a dystopian novel – drab brick buildings and trash and weeds and windows fogged over with layers of grime. The tree was my oasis from all of this ugliness.

Not long after my resignation, my principal cut the tree down. No more shade. No more oasis. It was almost comical.

I felt a little bit like a husband who has just gone through a divorce but his ex-wife has already found someone else to marry. The new man has moved in and they're sharing the master bedroom while I'm living in the unfinished basement. She feels pity for me and lets me stay there for now, but it would be easier for everyone if I just disappeared.

That's what my job felt like. They took away the one thing about work – coaching football – that I was really passionate about. My students thought I was radioactive.

And they cut down the tree outside of my classroom (I'm sure there was a perfectly good reason, but I was in a bad place, so *of course* the insult was intentional.)

I had done everything right. I had devoted myself to a cause that was bigger than me. I had put in the blood, sweat, and tears.

But sometimes, everything isn't enough. It took two years for this lesson to really sink in, but it has transformed the way I think about serving others.

I decided to come back to Jordan High School the following year. I could put on a noble face and say that I ultimately decided to be the bigger person, screw them, I wasn't going to let a bunch of parents run me out of town. But that wouldn't be true.

I thought about taking another teaching job. At a low point, I even decided to leave teaching all-together. I would go out on my own and do freelance editing full-time, even if it meant an unpredictable income and no health insurance benefits when I was the primary breadwinner and we had two little kids. I was so desperate to get out of my job that I was willing to risk everything.

My wife was a good sport about this mid-life crisis. She was patient and she listened to all of my complaining, even though alarms were probably going off in her head left and right.

Ultimately I walked back from the edge of the cliff.

But I dreaded the first day of the new school year. Without coaching, what was my professional identity going to be? Would my football players still talk to me, or would they resent my presence in the building? Would they even call me "Coach" anymore?

On that first day, I was stuck teaching a low-level sophomore English class first period. I hated world literature and I hated first period classes. I didn't want to be in this crumbling building anymore with a boss I didn't respect and a community that chewed me up and spit me out like an old race horse that needed to be put out to pasture. I was pissed off and self-righteous about all the ways the world was conspiring against me. I was deeply, deeply hurt.

And then that first period English class walked into my room. They were tough kids with hard faces – suspicious, kind of like me. And while they didn't come in with bright smiles and a great attitude, they didn't shut me out either. Neither did my football players. Many of them had even signed up for my creative writing classes. They still came to me for advice, and our conversations felt natural, like they wanted to be around me.

What was going on here? I wasn't sure. I didn't trust this tentative truce.

Weeks passed by. My low-level English class was full of undocumented immigrants, and as the 2016 presidential election grew closer, the fear began to rise in their faces. Were they going to get deported if Trump won? And when he did win, and a few people in our community were calling for all of the "dirty Mexicans" to go back where they came from, my students looked to me and wondered if all of this was true. Did they really belong here? Did America care about them? And what did I, as their teacher, think about all of this? Did *I* think they belonged here?

When you see vulnerability in a group of young people, especially young people who are conditioned to hide their vulnerability at all costs, it does something to you. Whatever personal baggage you are dealing with, whatever anger you've got stored inside of you, it all simply falls away when you come face to face with someone else's pain.

My baggage needed to fall away. Otherwise, what would that say about me? All of my anger and bitterness looked so small compared to these larger issues.

I was beginning to see what bitterness can do to a person's spirit. It consumes your heart and your head and feels like sludge in your veins. It weighs you down until you give in to it completely, destroying not only yourself but everyone you come in contact with.

So maybe this isn't a self-help book. But in spite of everything, I still believe that serving others is a transformative experience. We just need to approach it with open eyes and an open heart.

Even when your enemies try to cut you down to size.

Serving others is hard. It's also complicated. When you put yourself out there, you will be attacked. You will be ridiculed. You will be the man on stage alone with a hostile crowd throwing things at you.

I'm a big fan of the sociologist Brene Brown, whose research on shame and vulnerability has transformed the way I look at some of my lowest moments. Dr. Brown often refers to President Theodore Roosevelt's famous "Man in the Arena" speech, in which Roosevelt says, "It is not the critic who counts…The credit belongs to the man who is actually in the arena, whose face is marred by dust and sweat and blood; who strives valiantly; who errs, who comes short again and again…who spends himself in a worthy cause; who at the best knows in the end the triumph of high achievement, and who at the worst, if he fails, at least fails while daring greatly, so that his place shall never be with those cold and timid souls who neither know victory nor defeat."

My arena was a football field, with parents screaming from the stands. But this behavior is merely a reflection of our society. People are increasingly skeptical about institutions. Mainline church membership is declining. Public schools are under attack. Political parties have evolved into tribes that no longer speak to each other. It is *us* versus *them*, a climate where outrage is more common than civility.

My arena happened to be a public place, but the stakes can be very personal. When we serve others, we are invited into their brokenness. We absorb their stories, their pain, and their flaws. We *become* these things if we are not careful.

I have taught thousands of students over the years. It is a messy job because life is messy for so many of us. I have always struggled to keep this in perspective. How do I care about so many students without letting their struggles overwhelm me?

While I struggled to find my footing without football, I taught an advanced creative writing class. Every student in this class creates a book project, either a novel or a memoir. I've taught this class for over a decade, and it has always been inspiring to watch a group of teenagers struggle with an idea for an entire year and try to stick with that idea, even when their creativity runs dry. They learn the value of persistence by working on a project that has deep personal meaning to them. After a while, they don't care about their final grade in my class. It's no longer about the grade; it's about creating something that is lasting, something that they can look back on with pride. If schools could instill this idea across the curriculum, so many of our disconnected youth would be transformed.

I work closely with these kids, guiding them and cheering them on throughout the process. At any given time, I've got 25 storylines floating around in my head. Somehow it works. I forget many of my students' names after the year is up, but I never forget their stories.

One of my students was a girl named Beth. She sat in the corner and spoke with a very soft voice. I'd taught her the previous year, and she'd missed a lot of school for repeated hospitalizations. Beth's problems ran deep; she struggled with bulimia, suicidal thoughts, cutting, and lingering grief over the death of her father. Beth was a bright girl with a beautiful smile – a smile that rarely made it past the corners of her eyes.

At the suggestion of her therapist, Beth decided to write about her struggles with depression.

"Are you sure you want to do this?" I asked her, knowing that she would have to wrestle with this pain for an entire year.

Beth nodded her head firmly. "I think it will be good for me," she said. "And, you know, maybe it will help someone else who's going through this kind of thing."

For the rest of the year, Beth worked diligently on her memoir. I followed her progress and tried to give her focus when she needed it. Writing about her depression seemed to help. She started to smile more. She even began to date another boy in our class who was quiet like her, and kind too.

At the end of the year, I helped Beth to publish her memoir. She beamed with pride as she held the final book in her hand. I was proud of her too; Beth had written 38,000 brave and courageous words that documented some of the darkest moments in her life while ultimately providing a message of hope.

In the coming months after she graduated from high school, Beth was invited to speak at psychiatric hospitals about her experiences. Other girls found hope in her words, and this hope seemed to buoy Beth's spirits even more.

When Beth started college in the fall, many of us thought that she had conquered her pain. But depression is a horrible disease. It is ruthless and vile, and it can strike at any moment. It doesn't care about hope or redemption. It doesn't care about anything.

In September, Beth lost her battle with depression. She was in her bedroom at home when her mother found her, but it was too late.

How do you console a mother who has lost not only her husband but also a daughter? Beth was a triplet, and her sisters were devastated. They knew Beth was sick – they had always known it – but her suicide tore the family apart at the seams.

It was raining on the day of Beth's visitation. I drove to her house and parked behind a long line of cars. When I got to the house it was filled with family members and friends. I hugged Beth's sisters, who had both taken my creative writing class the previous year. They were quiet girls like Beth, kind and caring sisters. I spoke to their mother as well, along with her grandfather, a retired pastor who held himself together with a quiet dignity that was heartbreaking.

After the visitation, I sat in my car and watched the rain fall down my windshield. I cried so hard that my shoulders started shaking.

Death is never easy, but the death of a child is particularly cruel. Over the years I have built up armor to protect myself against losses like this. Fortunately, I haven't been in this situation very often, but it has happened more than I care to admit.

A few years back, one of my students lost his life to gang violence. Another former student was shot and killed more recently. This one hit me harder because he was the father of a seven-year-old boy, the same age as my son Brett.

Since I've been at the same school for 17 years, I've also seen the long-term effects of poverty and crime on certain families. In my first year of teaching at Jordan High School, one of my football players, Vincent, was convicted of rape and kidnapping. His younger brother Shaq was five when it happened. Recently Shaq was a student in my class, and he could vividly remember going to see his older brother play football before the arrest. These memories were precious because they were some of the only snapshots of his brother out of prison, where Vincent is serving a twenty-year sentence.

I also taught Vincent's sister Jordyn. She was a little older than Shaq and a bit more introspective. In class, she wrote vivid stories about talking to Vincent in prison, about the loss of it all, the way his hair was already turning gray and their conversations were getting more and more forced, because how could he really understand what her family was going through? When Vincent was convicted of that horrible crime so many years ago, his family lost a good bit of their freedom as well.

For over a decade I have witnessed the effects of incarceration on this family. Jordyn's self-esteem plummeted and she sought validation in relationships with shady men, ultimately giving birth to three kids with three different men before she turned 22. Shaq struggled as well. He quit football and started dealing drugs. He stopped coming to school.

One day Shaq and an older cousin were hanging out in Rockwood Park. This park was one of my favorite places to take Brett and Cason in the heat of the summer because it was shaded by large oak trees, and it had a playground with a good loop for riding bikes. I'd taken my boys there earlier in the week.

Shaq and his cousin were standing in the parking lot when a car pulled up and opened fire. Shaq's cousin was killed instantly, and Shaq took several bullets to the stomach. He survived, but he walked with a permanent limp afterwards. Beneath one of the oak trees in the park, family and friends made a shrine of flowers and cards in honor of Shaq's cousin. It rained a few days after the murder. When I took Brett and

Cason to play in the park, the flowers had already wilted away and the ink had bled through the cards.

What will happen to Shaq in the future? Will I be around long enough to teach his future kids, or Jordyn's kids? Will they ever be able to break out of the cycle of poverty and brokenness?

These questions can eat away at you if you're not careful. They can make you question the goodness of the world. They can drive you to pessimism and despair.

What does it all mean? Why is the world so broken and so hopeless? Why was I lucky enough to avoid this kind of trauma as a kid?

When I think about people like Beth and Shaq, I feel ashamed of my own childhood sadness. I was incredibly lucky; my life could have been so much more difficult. And even now, being fully aware of how lucky I am, I recognize how difficult it can be to build relationships with people who are broken.

It is so much easier to stay in our own protective bubble. We don't have to deal with depression (we are only lying to ourselves). We don't have to deal with brokenness (it is still there even if we choose to ignore it). We can control the world and bend it to our will (even though the world doesn't care about our best-laid plans).

Life is messy. Caring about other people is messy. We need to acknowledge this before we go about the work of serving others.

It is hard to step into someone's brokenness without drowning in it. But this kind of work has to be done. There is beauty amidst the brokenness. There is goodness in the most hardened individuals. We can choose to stay out of the arena. We can avoid the criticism and the discomfort and the sadness of it all. Or we can dive in.

What does this shift look like?

Before we go any further, we need a working definition of service.

The Oxford Dictionary defines service as "the action of helping or doing work for someone." *Merriam-Webster* defines service as "help, use, benefit" and the "contribution to the welfare of others."

Service has its roots in the Latin word "servitium," meaning slave. This is obviously problematic in our modern context. At its worst, a slave has historically been someone who is bought and sold as property. In more contemporary usage, the word occasionally describes a person who works very hard without earning enough money or appreciation for his/her efforts.

I've always been interested in the way that words have evolved over time. I know this is the English nerd in me, but this interest also stems from my three years of Latin in high school. I originally took Latin because it is a dead language and I knew that I wouldn't have to speak it out loud. Then I got into the class and discovered that so much of modern

English has its origins in a core set of Latin roots and phrases. This blew me away. I started to trace the evolution of words over time as they constantly took on new meanings. Sometimes this evolution came from cultural and social upheavals. Other times it seemed to come randomly. This could happen at the speed of sound. In just 17 years of teaching, teens stopped saying *cool* and tried on everything from *banging* to *clutch*, *dope*, *crunk*, *phat*, *off da hook*, *tight*, and most recently, *lit*. Although I'm certain that *lit* will be out of fashion by the time this book is published.

And so it goes with the definition of service. When we serve others, we usually don't think about the concept of slavery. We *choose* to help someone else. No one forces us to do it. But we do value appreciation for our efforts. This is not the primary reason we serve others, but it speaks to our need for validation.

We really, truly want to do good in the world. But we also want someone to point out that they see us doing good. Why isn't the act itself enough? This speaks to our weakness as a species. All of us have a desire to be good. We crave it. We need to be good in order to live a joyful life. For many of us, this is all the motivation we need. Our goodwill is like a cup that spills over or runs dry at various stages of our lives. I want my cup to stay full, and I hope that by folding outwards into the world, by serving others and by focusing on something other than myself, perhaps my cup will never run dry.

And still, in spite of my best intentions, my cup runs dry. Someone has to lift me up from time to time. I wish it didn't work like that. Maybe I can learn to live another way.

Serving others is hard. In fact, I would argue that it is impossible to do this kind of work without a certain set of character traits. Sure, you can fake it for a while, and you can even do some good along the way. But if you really want to help others – if you want to do it joyfully and with an open heart for years to come – you need to have some, if not all, of the following traits:

1. Comfortable in your own skin
2. Empathetic
3. Self-directed
4. Low-drama
5. You have to like people
6. Hard-working
7. Able to live in the here and now
8. Capable of long-range thinking
9. You need to have leadership ability (and no, this doesn't mean that you have to dominate a room)
10. Humility

This is not an exhaustive list by any means. And I am certainly no expert on the human psyche – I'll leave that to researchers with a much higher pay grade.

But I believe in these traits. They have guided me through the wilderness on any number of occasions. It is worth thinking about these traits and asking ourselves the following question: Is it hard for me to embody any of these ten qualities?

These traits are the armor that will sustain us when we serve others. They are the interconnected system of roots, the pumping veins, the firm foundation. It has taken me years to develop these qualities, and I continue to be a work in progress. All of us, if we are true to ourselves, are a constant work in progress.

But we don't have to stand in place. We can grow. We can evolve. Thinking about this list has been a vital part of my evolution. I hope it can be helpful to you as well.

#1
Comfortable in Your Own Skin

Isabella didn't trust me at all. She didn't trust most people, but she really didn't want to be in my English class at 9:00 every morning.

She made this abundantly clear with her body language – lots of eye rolling and slouching in her desk (in the back of the room, of course.) But I've taught long enough to know that this was mainly an act. Isabella was incredibly smart. I was planning to call her on this; I just needed to get her to trust me first. That's kind of my thing. I like to challenge my students and get a rise out of them. I don't mind them arguing back at me, but I always wait until I have built some kind of connection first. Once a kid knows you are genuine and you care about them, you can call them on their bullshit every single time. They will smile knowingly, as if the two of you are in on the same joke.

But I wasn't there yet with Isabella. She was a hard egg to crack.

At the beginning of class, I introduced an activity on sensory details. My whiteboard was divided into five segments, with each segment representing one of the five senses – sight of … smell of … and so on. To get the activity started, I began to write an example for each sense:

The smell of fall leaves.

The sound of a Boston subway train.

I have a hard time focusing on multiple things at once. I lock in to a task at hand with hyper-focus, which can be a good thing, but when you're teaching a class of 29 cut-ups it can also be a major weakness.

I was talking and writing at the same time, which usually ends poorly for me.

The taste of sweat tea, I wrote.

Isabella stopped twirling her hair. "*Sweat* tea?"

"What?" I asked.

"You wrote *sweat* tea. What the hell is sweat tea?"

"*Sweet* tea," I said, correcting the spelling in my head.

"Yeah, but you wrote *sweat* tea."

The other kids were awake now. Isabella was challenging me. This could get interesting.

I thought about bluffing, about pretending that I hadn't made the error. *Sweet tea versus sweat tea, who gives a shit?* I could point out that none of her classmates cared enough to point out the error. *I'm a good speller! Better than you, Isabella, with your typos scattered throughout your otherwise brilliant writing.* I had every right to get defensive.

Instead, I started laughing. And just like that, Isabella was laughing right along with me. So was the rest of the class. I became human to them for the first time. We were all in on the same joke.

In the months to come, Isabella would become one of my most enthusiastic students. That one incident completely bridged the gap between us. And none of it would have happened if I hadn't been comfortable in my own skin.

Kids have a unique ability to spot sincerity. They will love you for it. They can also tell when you are being fake – and when they see you being fake, they will eat you alive.

I wasn't always comfortable in my own skin. As a kid I was never tall enough, handsome enough, worthy enough of someone's love. When I first became a head football coach, I tried to imitate how I thought a head coach was supposed to act. I'd scream and berate players during practice. I never smiled. During the halftime of games, instead of offering clear instructions for how we could win, I yelled and tried to get guys hyped up, as if emotion was the solution to every problem. But I never felt comfortable acting like this because it wasn't me. Our team suffered because I wasn't brave enough to be myself. When I finally realized this, I enjoyed coaching a whole lot more. My players could sense it, and they played with more focus and control. They could tell that I was leading from an authentic place.

This comfort happened slowly over time, forged by confidence and the reality that life is not about me.

This is who I am.

You have to own this image of yourself. People will respect you for it, especially when you own up to your mistakes.

When someone shows their vulnerability to us, we feel emboldened to be vulnerable right back to them. My best classes have always been the ones in which a student takes that first bold step to show a group of strangers who he/she really is. Nothing is ever the same after that. It takes courage to make that initial step, but it has a snowball effect on a larger group.

The next time you watch a comedy routine, I want you to think about the kinds of jokes that get the most laughs. It won't be the mean-spirited comments about some group of people. The best comedians (and the best public speakers, for that matter) know that the surest way to win over an audience is to make fun of themselves. This is vulnerability hidden beneath humor, but it is still vulnerability. As someone in the audience, we are immediately put at ease. This speaker is brave. We can relate to them. They make mistakes too, and they are able to show their flaws in a public way, with the lights shining down upon them. This takes guts. It is inspiring.

I love my current principal for the same set of reasons. She's all out there. When she's having a good day, she lets us know. When she's angry, we know that as well. You might think this would make us uncomfortable, but it doesn't.

Isn't she supposed to be the stable one? you might ask. *The rock? Principals aren't allowed to show emotion, are they?*

But I'll tell you why she is an effective principal: she is consistent. This is who she is. And she is comfortable in that dynamic. She wants us to know when she is happy so that we can celebrate all of the good things we are doing at this school. She doesn't show her anger as a way of shaming or embarrassing us. Instead, it is a challenge for us to be better teachers. When she screws up, she tells us that as well. Now if she screwed up all the time, we would lose respect for her after a while. But if someone stands before a group of 100 teachers and admits to being human, we are likely to respect this person.

Now think about your favorite politician. It could be our president, or a state senator, or even your local city council member. When they screw up, how do you want them to act? Should they cover it up? Should they place the blame on someone else? Or should they simply own up to their mistakes? Will you lose any respect for them if they apologize for being human? Probably not. Deep down, we see vulnerability as an act of bravery. When we see someone owning their true selves, warts and all, we are inspired to be comfortable in our own skin.

How can we possibly serve others if we do not own the skin that we inhabit? We can't – at least not for long, and definitely not in an authentic way.

When we are comfortable in our own skin, we free ourselves to think about others.

#2
Empathy

So what does it mean to think about others? Partly this is a matter of curiosity. I love to watch people when I'm out in public. Coffee shops are some of my favorite spots, but any public space will do. The point is to observe people, not to disturb them. You want to blend into the background. Whenever I see an interesting person, I try to imagine their life story. Where do they come from? What are their hopes and dreams? Why do they seem so happy or so serious? Happy and sad people are equally fascinating to me. I don't see their baggage as something to be ashamed of. Instead, I am interested in the countless moments that have led to this very day where I, a complete stranger, get to watch another stranger simply be alive.

I do this, in part, because I like to tell stories. And let's be honest here: we all want to live a good story. We want a challenge to overcome, a person to rescue, a happy-ever-after ending. More than anything, we want to be seen in the world. We want our lives to hold value, both to ourselves and to others. This is a constant struggle, the give and take between how much we can lift ourselves up and how much we need others to do the heavy lifting for us.

Most of the time we simply can't do this on our own; we need other people. But it is impossible to connect with someone if we do not understand them on a deeper level. We have to show them empathy.

Empathy is the ability to understand and share the feelings of another. Empathy calls us to honestly look at another human being and to imagine their story in all of its complexity. We have to see the world from their point of view instead of our own.

In her book *Beyond the Beautiful Forevers*, the journalist Katherine Boo writes, "I don't try to fool myself that the stories of individuals are themselves arguments. I just believe that better arguments, maybe even better policies, get formulated when we know more about ordinary lives."

The problem comes when we look at an "ordinary" person and we struggle to see beneath the surface. We pass judgment. We pull from our own life experiences and reflect our own world view upon them. We make them a character in *our* story instead of seeing them as a rich and complex character in their own epic novel.

This work is hard for us. And it becomes more difficult every year, as we grow further entrenched in our respective groups.

I am as guilty as anyone. For many years, one group of students has eluded my understanding the most: our immigrant population. During the 17 years that I have taught at my current school, our English as a Second Language (ESL) Program has more than doubled. In addition to a large increase in students from Latin America, we have seen significant population increases from Africa, Vietnam, and, most recently, from war-torn countries such as Syria. And while our school has done an admirable job of meeting the needs of our growing immigrant population, I have not always done a very good job of engaging these students.

In recent years I have decided to change this. Instead of looking at these students as "foreigners" or simply "the other," I have made a concerted effort to get to know them as people with rich, complex stories.

In the fall of 2016, I led a group of students from across the district in an after-school program called Teen NaNoWriMo (short for National Novel Writing Month), a designated time when people from all across the world make a pledge to write a book in a single month. Typically this challenge is reserved for adults, but I wanted to encourage young people to try it as well.

One of the participants was Rocky, who happened to be a student in my 11th grade English class at the time. She was quiet and guarded; until that month, I had only spoken to her a handful of times. I did not even realize she was passionate about writing until she showed up to the first afternoon session. But as the days passed by, Rocky opened up to me through her words.

I learned that Rocky was undocumented, having arrived in America at the age of six with little to no knowledge of English. She left Honduras after her brother was murdered. A *coyote* smuggled Rocky into Texas and handed her off to another smuggler, who kidnapped Rocky and held her in his basement for two weeks until Rocky's mother could come up with the ransom money (because her mother was also undocumented, notifying the police was out of the question.)

So for two weeks, Rocky sat alone in a dark basement. She survived on stale bread and water. Every time she heard feet shuffling overhead, she thought she was going to be killed.

The more I learned about Rocky's past, the more I admired her courage and resilience. But I felt ashamed, too. On the first day of school, I noticed the tattoos on her knuckles and the "hard" look on her face, and I immediately pegged her as a problem student. I was completely wrong.

Rocky was an honors student. She was bright and inquisitive, qualities that were hard for people like me to see because she was also very quiet. She didn't smile much because her life wasn't easy. Every day she knew that ICE agents could show up at her doorstep and take her parents away. They could take her away too. Life was a never-ending cycle of appearing and then disappearing into the shadows.

I never would have known about any of this if Rocky hadn't opened up to me.

I saw Rocky's tattooed fingers and her constant scowl as a direct affront to me. I thought of her as a character in my story instead of the other way around. I was just a minor character in her story – and what an incredibly complex story it was.

Writing had become Rocky's passion. If there is any gift that we can give a young person, it is to help them find a purpose in their daily life. But it has to be *their* purpose and not our own. This requires us to see them in 3D. With empathy.

Student success, I have come to believe, has little to do with ability and everything to do with purpose. Once a student finds a driving interest during the school day, that interest will inevitably push them to be curious about the world outside of their daily experiences. And once a student sees just how big the world is, they are more likely to become an active participant in the world in meaningful ways. They want to take on adult responsibilities. They want to learn from people who come from diverse backgrounds. In short, they want to make a positive impact on the world.

When I look at my students, I try to see the innate goodness in all of them. If I can guide them in some small way to find their passions, then I have done my job. Students like Rocky give me hope for the future. They remind me that goodness can spring from our darkest places and our greatest fears.

I try to remember that while our own stories are worthwhile, there are many other beautiful stories floating around us. If we could only amplify these stories to the world, lifting up the courage of others instead of dwelling on our own insecurities, we would live in a culture of celebration rather than fear. A shadow scares us because it forces us to jump to our defenses, imagining a threat that is not really there and is never as imposing as the object it reflects. So it is with the people we see around us. If you don't know someone's story, you are bound to create a story that is flawed and influenced by the unknown.

Rocky's story is more dramatic than most. Most of the people we come into contact with haven't come to this country under the cover of night. They haven't come face to face with death or found themselves in the midst of a national political debate.

But that doesn't make them any less important.

When you show empathy for people, you begin to see how much we all have in common. We want to be loved. We want to be happy. We want to matter in some small way, whether it's to our parents or to our local community. We are deeply connected to the fabric of other people.

Living with empathy is like seeing the world in color for the first time. We become curious about other people, no matter who they are or where they are from.

When I watch someone get off of an airplane, I immediately try to create their story in my head. This has always been interesting to me. The difference is, I used to filter their hypothetical experiences through the lens of my own experiences. Now I try to be more open-minded. *Who are they really?* I ask myself. *What are the possibilities?*

If we look outward with empathy, we will see things that have always been there – we are just now recognizing them for the first time.

One Saturday in May, I was walking with my wife and two sons beside a lake. People were all around us, going about their lives, flying kites or relaxing on the shore or speaking loudly into their cell phones. It would be easy to focus on my immediate surroundings and let everyone else blur into the background. Sometimes we have to do that; otherwise the world can feel all-consuming.

But today I tried to be fully present. I wanted to experience everything – the gentle wind, the sun, the laughter of my children, and my wife's warm hand in mine.

Up ahead, I saw a teenage boy pacing beside the lake. He wore a dark suit that was a couple sizes too big. His tie was a bit crooked. On my second loop around the lake, I saw him again, still pacing, still looking at his watch from time to time. This time I noticed the gazebo behind him, where he had set up a table for two. There were flowers and candles on the table. He had made a sign that said, "Will you go to prom with me?"

I smiled to myself, glad that I wasn't in high school anymore.

On my third lap around the lake, the boy was no longer pacing back and forth. He was slumped over the table, his head in his hands. Clearly, the girl wasn't going to show up.

What was this boy's story? Perhaps he was a hopeless romantic. Maybe he never really had a chance with the girl. Who knows. But there was definitely a story there. That boy mattered. And the girl – whoever she was and wherever she was at that moment instead of eating dinner with him – she mattered too. She also had a story to tell.

I never found out the real story. In order to show empathy, we don't necessarily need to know the full story. But we do have to believe that the story exists. When we see people for who they are and who they can be, we exist in a world outside of ourselves.

This is a much better world to live in.

We have to see people for who they are.

But what do we do about people who are hard to like? This is a very real challenge. People can be pessimistic, bigoted, rude, and just plain cruel. It can be hard to see the goodness in someone like that. But that's okay. When someone says something that we disagree with, we don't have to mount an immediate defense. Believe me, I want to mount an immediate defense, especially when I know that someone's opinion is factually wrong. But then I have to ask myself if this person's ignorance is worth my time and energy and the headache that is beginning to appear. Usually the answer is no. If that person is attacking someone who is weak or defenseless, that is a whole different story. We have a moral responsibility to defend the helpless. But we don't have a moral responsibility to argue with every idiot who has a half-baked opinion.

Sometimes we have to be realistic. People will always let us down, because brokenness is one of the most basic parts of humanity. And there *is* such a thing as evil. Some people seem to be broken beyond redemption. But most of the time, we give the people who anger us more power than they deserve. People lash out when they are broken. They try to inflict pain on others because they are consumed with pain.

I think of the single mom who wanted to get me fired because her son wasn't getting enough playing time in football. She wanted to hurt me. She'd glare at me with a level of hatred that made my skin crawl. But she didn't really hate me. She hated what I represented. She was probably struggling to keep her life together while her son was getting involved with the wrong crowd, skipping classes and making her worry about what was going to happen to him in the future. He was all she had – she had told me as much (with a few extra insults thrown at me for good measure.) She saw me as an obstacle to her son's happiness. That didn't make it right, but it did make it real. She didn't give a damn about me or about what getting fired would do to my family.

When I looked at her through this new lens, most of my anger fell away. I still didn't like her; I was never going to like her. But I could finally see that this whole stupid drama was not about me. I wasn't doing anything unethical, so my job wasn't on the line. I had to put up with some unpleasant conversations with this mother and my principal, but the matter was dropped after a while.

I let the whole situation sit in my heart for much longer than it should have. I gave this mother that power over me.

So empathy is not just about loving people. It is not even about serving people. Empathy is about seeing people for who they really are. If we look at people with empathy, we will inevitably see the world in a better light.

Cast aside the bad. Focus on the good. This is such a simple way to live. It is not always easy, but it can be a revolutionary act.

#3
Self-direction

I am a big believer in moderation. Unfortunately, people don't get excited about the spaces in between a debate. There's nothing sexy about compromise, or nuance, or seeing both sides of an issue. We'd rather have black and white. Perhaps it is simply part of our DNA; uncertainty scares us.

When it comes to what drives individual success, people tend to fall into two camps:

Camp 1: Success is the product of individual responsibility.

Camp 2: Success is directly related to our environment.

This is the classic nature versus nurture debate, which has been ongoing since the days of the Greek philosophers.

I fall firmly in the middle of this debate. Our environment matters, whether it's the family we were born into, the region of the country where we grew up, the quality of our schools, the color of our skin, our gender, or our sexual orientation. All of these things weigh heavily on our lives.

But I also believe in the merits of personal responsibility. Again and again in my teaching career, I've taught siblings who have gone down drastically different paths in life, despite living under the same roof and getting pretty much the same parental guidance. For example, sibling #1 goes off to Columbia University for college while sibling #2 drops out of high school and becomes an exotic dancer. Or in another real case, sibling #1 becomes a convicted felon while sibling #2 becomes a police officer. These kinds of differences happen all the time with the families I work with.

We can't discount the freedom of our individual decisions. Otherwise, why get up in the morning? If we are simply coasting along a pre-ordained path, then life would be meaningless. A life of privilege would feel empty. On the flip side, growing up in a life of poverty and seemingly insurmountable obstacles could easily make someone give up without even trying.

In fact, if we buy into the argument that our environment controls everything, then this list of ten character traits wouldn't even be worth exploring. You could look at the previous two sections and say, "Either you're comfortable in your skin or you're not. Either you understand empathy or you don't."

Obviously I disagree with this way of thinking.

These ten character traits are not only important, but they can be developed over time. The growing scientific field of Neuroplasticity – the ability of the brain to change throughout an individual's life – speaks to this phenomenon. The latest research tells us that it's never too late to learn something new, to grow, or to change our way of thinking. Sure, we become set in our ways as we get older, but we can always change who we are for the better, no matter what age we decide to make that change. I would argue that as we get older, it is essential that we continue to learn new things and to see the world in new ways.

About ten years ago, my dad suffered a stroke that affected his ability to speak, causing his words to come out slow and halting. It also caused him to get disoriented easily and to lose his balance. It was heartbreaking to watch this change. My dad always had an incredibly sharp wit, a good memory, and the logical brain of a successful lawyer. After the stroke, I thought he had lost all of this.

I didn't know how to help my dad. I wasn't a doctor, and I didn't have enough money to really help him out with rehabilitative care.

But I was a writer. So I encouraged my dad to write his life story. For the first time in his life, he sat down at a computer to write something about himself. It was messy at first, filled with odd formatting and thoughts that jumped from one stage of his life to the next. But my dad stuck with it. The discipline gave him a sense of purpose. It also gave him a voice when his own slurred speech left him red-faced with frustration. In the coming months, my dad's writing got clearer. So did his thoughts. When he was 15 years old, he was diagnosed with testicular cancer. At the time (1964), this diagnosis was basically a death sentence. My grandparents flew him up to New York for an emergency surgery, with little hope that he would live another year. When I was growing up, my dad rarely talked about this time in his life. But through his writing, I found a new window into his past.

"The morning of the surgery was gorgeous in New York City," my dad wrote. "The air was clear and you could see the sun rising over the East River through the seventh floor hospital window. The ornate bridges crossing the East River stood tall carrying the City's traffic."

I shook my head as I read these words from a man who, just months before, could barely speak and wrote disjointed sentences in 20-point font that were filled with lawyerly jargon. The process of writing seemed to be rewiring his brain. The old Alan Albright started to come back. His slurred speech eventually became normal again. His balance improved. I'm sure that it was more than just the writing, but finding a purpose had clearly improved my dad's quality of life.

I'm glad that I could help my dad. But ultimately, he did this on his own. He made the decision to lean in to a really crappy situation and to do something about it. He made a personal decision that, while influenced by his upbringing and the support he received from his family, ultimately came down to one man, sitting in a wheelchair and deciding that he wasn't ready to give up just yet.

In order to serve others, we have to be self-directed. As I mentioned earlier, putting others first can be messy. It's hard to lift someone up when no one gives you credit for your efforts. At every step along the way, we have to acknowledge our flaws, our selfish tendencies, our constant desire for affirmation. Very few people can be completely selfless without getting something in return. That *something* doesn't have to be a pat on the back or money or attention, but we do need to feel like we have value and are valued by those we serve.

Service sits firmly in the murky ground between our environment and personal responsibility. We have to make an individual decision to help someone else. But we also need to be aware of our environment. Why do we want to serve? What need is not being met in our community? Is service merely a part of our own selfish ambitions? Or do we serve because somewhere deep in the best part of our soul – in the place that is pure and good but often suppressed by the Seduction of the Self – we know that putting other people first is the surest way to find joy in this world?

This work is hard. It requires courage too. Serving others often means that we have to fight against an entire culture's way of thinking. People will look at us like we are crazy. Or more likely, they will simply ignore us. And that's probably a good thing. Otherwise we will have to wrestle with the public acknowledgement of our "good deeds" and all of the baggage that goes along with it.

When you serve others, you will often find yourself alone. You will be uncomfortable and scared. You will wonder if you are making the right decisions. It won't matter where you came from. It won't matter what privileges or obstacles you've faced in the past. You will be on a stage by yourself with the world staring back, daring you to fall in line, daring you to take the easy way out.

The easy way isn't evil; in fact, that's what makes it so tempting. The easy way is predictable. Your friends are there. Security is there. Affirmation is there.

To be a free thinker is to be lonely. Going against the tide requires every bit of personal integrity that you can muster.

***

On two different occasions, I have wrestled with this kind of loneliness.

I have to be completely honest: it sucks to be lonely.

The first time I faced this kind of loneliness was in college. I had just finished up my sophomore year, and I got a job for the summer working at a youth center in Camden, New Jersey. Camden is often called America's poorest city. It lies less than a mile across the Delaware River from downtown Philadelphia, but it might as well be another planet away. Camden is a city plagued by bankruptcy, political corruption, and violent crime. The youth center where I worked was located on the waterfront, next to a garbage dump and a medical waste facility that burned amputated body parts. If the smell of death had a name, it would be Camden.

I didn't know anyone in Camden, so I rented a room from a stranger. Every morning I drove a beat-up van around the city, picking up kids for the summer program and then teaching them the rest of the day. I also picked up food for their lunches, worked in the soup kitchen next to the youth center, and ended my day by driving the same kids home as the sun went down. It was exhausting, exhilarating work that forced me to always live in the moment. I knew that I was doing real work to help these kids, who desperately needed love and support. This was service in the purest sense.

But it was also incredibly lonely work. My friends were home in North Carolina working at internships or simply lounging around, being typical 20 year olds. I felt like I had stepped into a world beyond anything I had known before. Every day I found myself questioning why I was there, even in those moments when I knew that I was doing the right thing.

At the end of every long day, I felt my body give in to the constant smell of decaying garbage and incinerated body parts. The Philadelphia area was in the midst of one of the worst heat waves in decades, and the temperature was suffocating. I got in my car and drove down unfamiliar streets to my little room in a neighborhood that would never feel like home. I ate my microwave dinner in silence or went to a nearby mall just so I could be around other people.

I was sad for much of those three months in Camden. I was completely out of my comfort zone. No friends, no family, nothing to anchor me.

But I constantly reminded myself why I was there in the first place. I wanted to make a tangible difference in the lives of other people. I *chose* to be up there. Nobody made me do it. In fact, most of the people I knew told me *not* to come up there: "How is a job like this going to look on your resume?" they seemed to be saying. "Think of all the missed networking opportunities! The lost career capital!" And the most common question of all: "How much good can you *really* do in three short months?"

I never once thought about quitting while I lived in Camden. I made that choice on my own. Perhaps it was dumb luck that I stuck it out, but that dumb luck gave me a taste of service. It showed me the power that a teacher can have in the life of a young person. If I hadn't made the decision to step out of my comfort zone, I would probably be following my father's footsteps as a lawyer. There's nothing wrong with being a lawyer, but it would have been a career decision based off of nothing more than familiarity.

I didn't grow up wanting to be a teacher. Seventeen years into this profession, I still don't know for sure if this is the one career that I am destined for. But it fits just fine. My career choice is a by-product of my desire to serve others. That orientation is important. We have to start with a simple goal, with a clear end in sight. Then we have to travel down this road whether it is crowded or empty. It doesn't matter who else is out there. Other drivers can distract us or get in the way, but we can't give them the power to tell us what our final destination will be.

The second time I wrestled with this kind of loneliness was immediately after graduating from college.

I turned down a chance to stay at UNC Chapel Hill for graduate school and moved to Boston instead. Harvard University's teaching program had recently changed its focus to inner-city education. That was appealing to me. Plus, it was Harvard. I know that sounds selfish, but as a public school kid from the South, I had the sneaking suspicion that Harvard must have admitted me by mistake. I needed to enroll quickly before they realized their error.

So three weeks after graduating from UNC, I was back in school.

Harvard's teaching program is incredibly intense. You complete a master's degree in one calendar year. At the same time you teach pretty much the full year in one of Boston's public high schools. I figured that since I was already signed up to work in an urban education program, I might as well volunteer to do my student teaching in one of the lowest-performing schools in the district: Boston English High School.

Like Camden, Boston was a challenging place to work. English High School used to be an old factory building. It was overcrowded and chaotic, with some of the poorest students in the city. The 9/11 attacks happened the year I was up there, and I remember the tension amongst my students for months afterward – the random attacks on Muslims in the subway, the Somali refugees at my school who were nearly beaten to death for wearing the hijab. Kids brought guns to school and pulled fire alarms and set bulletin boards on fire. I taught incredible kids too, like the refugee from Rwanda who was the only person in her family to survive an attack on her village. She hid in the brush while her family was slaughtered and then walked hundreds of miles to get to a border camp. Somehow she found her way to Boston and the chance at a better life.

The year was a blur of lesson planning and discipline headaches, followed by classes at Harvard every afternoon. My head was swimming so much from my experiences at English High that I often failed to appreciate the world-class education I was getting at Harvard. But I have vivid images of beauty too: taking the T across the Charles River in the afternoon and watching the setting sun bring downtown Boston to life; the salty smell of a New England winter; the old brownstone buildings and the history of the city, everything moving with a constant hustle and bustle that was so different from what I had known in North Carolina. I loved to walk along the Charles River near my tiny apartment, watching the Harvard crew teams rowing silently in the fall, and the snow creeping along the banks of the river as November turned to December.

I felt alive that year in Boston. Cold, exhausted, sleep-deprived … but alive.

That doesn't mean I was always happy. In fact, it's possible to feel alive while simultaneously wrestling with incredible loneliness.

One of my favorite books is *Into the Wild* by Jon Krakauer. I read it right before I moved up to Boston, and it speaks to this dual state of being completely alive while still struggling to find meaning. *Into the Wild* tells the fascinating story of Christopher McCandless, who gave away everything he owned after graduating from college and hitch-hiked across the country. He eventually found his way deep into the Alaska wilderness, where he starved to death while living in an abandoned school bus. The book traces McCandless's journey through a stack of journals and other books that he left behind. In many ways, McCandless found exactly what he was looking for – complete freedom – but in the final weeks of his life he seemed to have a change of heart. He decided to return to civilization, but a swollen river blocked his exit out of the wilderness.

At the end of his life, McCandless wrote the following sentence in the margins of a Tolstoy book he was reading: "Happiness is only real when shared."

These words came back to me near the end of my year in Boston. Who was I sharing my happiest moments with? I'd made good friends at Harvard, but we were all heading to different parts of the country at the end of the year.

Then there was my girlfriend back home in North Carolina. We'd been together for three years, off and on. Things seemed to be getting serious, but what does serious really look like to a 22-year-old? Were we supposed to find jobs in the same city? Move in together? Or should we just continue this long-distance relationship indefinitely?

I was becoming more and more comfortable with the idea of living on my own. I wasn't afraid to take risks, like moving to a completely new city. Camden and Boston had taught me that. But I was starting to see that being *self-directed* was not the same thing as being *selfish*. I had to make some decisions that would shape every aspect of my life to come. I needed some clarity.

Long distance doesn't help you clarify anything. Every night I'd sit on the window ledge of my fire escape, dutifully talking to my girlfriend on the phone. Her voice sounded so far away. "Are you okay?" I'd say again and again. "You sound sad … Of course I still love you … We don't have to plan out the rest of our lives tonight."

I rubbed my weary eyes and talked in circles, night after night.

Happiness is only real when shared ... I wasn't sure what to think of that quote as the spring semester came to a close.

Eventually I made some choices. I took a job back home in North Carolina. My girlfriend moved to New York. I settled into my new life as a teacher and football coach, diligently calling her every night after 9:00 pm. Like most new teachers, I worked ridiculously long hours. I gave everything I had to my job. Then I tried to give all that was left to a girl on the phone 500 miles away.

"I love you, Stu," my girlfriend finally said. "But I'm not sure if I'm *in love* with you anymore."

That was it. Right then and there we ended things over the phone, hung up, and never spoke to each other again.

Life has a way of pivoting on little moments like this – moments that seem so small at the time but leave lasting imprints. A single phone call. A decision to move to North Carolina instead of New York. A father spending time with his son at a Friday night football game. A student who smiles in the midst of unspeakable struggles. Sadness. Happiness. Embarrassment. Everything adds up to define our future. If we're smart, we'll pay attention long enough to see these moments for what they really are: the nudges that send our lives in a completely different direction from where they started.

After that break-up, it took me a while to stitch my heart back together. But even in the midst of my grieving, I felt clarity for the first time in years. I was in control of my life. And if I was going to continue serving people with an open spirit, I needed to find a better balance between sacrificing myself for others, or sharing my life with those who were receptive to the love I was offering.

Either way, we all have to choose. These choices can be easy, but they can also be very difficult. They can affect our lives for years to come. But in the end I would rather live without regrets. I would rather love with open arms and a full heart.

I wish the same thing for my ex-girlfriend, whatever she's doing and wherever life has taken her since that final phone call. Twenty years have gone by. I hope she is married to someone who loves her and treats her well. I hope she has kids who fill her with joy the way my two sons fill me with joy. Above all, I hope she is happy. That's all we can ask of the people who cross our paths in both small and significant ways. I hope that I was good to her. I hope that I've been good to all of my friends and loved ones throughout time.

And to those I haven't met yet, I hope to be good to you as well. After all, the choice is mine to make.

#4

Low Drama

I am an affectionate person. I like to hug friends when I see them. If someone does something that is especially brave or kind, I make a big deal out of it. I wear my heart on my sleeve, and I'm not ashamed to be this way.

But there is a difference between authentic affection and a public demonstration of affection.

I'd rather hide in a hole than attend my own birthday party. I loved my wedding ceremony but I felt out of place at the reception afterward. I can't stand the public make-out sessions in the hallway outside my classroom, or the elaborate and intentionally cheesy "promposals" that teenage boys have to suffer through these days. I'm suspicious of public demonstrations like this because they tend to come from a place of awkwardness or insecurity. The girl eating her boyfriend's face against the school wall isn't more in love than the other couples at school. The beauty of a prom night or a wedding isn't predicated on the "right" words of the proposal. No act is truly genuine unless it comes from the heart. Not from precedent, or the latest trend, or what we think we have to do. We need to just do it.

Merriam-Webster defines drama as "a state, situation, or series of events involving an interesting or intense conflict of forces." *Drama* originates from the Greek word *dran*, meaning to "do or act."

And so we act.

Life can be boring and tedious, so we look for ways to break up the tedium. Nobody runs the other way when we see a fight. We are drawn to it. These days even that isn't enough; we have to document the moment with our cameras. We do this so that others may bear witness to our unique experience (or simply to gloat about how interesting our lives have become.)

So *drama* means "to do or act" – which, more often than not, means to act like a fool.

Just this spring, one of my students got upset because another dude was feeding strawberries to his girlfriend in the cafeteria. This could have been handled any number of ways. He could have told himself that this was probably a lie or, at the very least, a stretch of the truth. After all, show me the teenage boy who actually feeds fruit to another guy's girlfriend in a greasy school cafeteria. Wouldn't it be pizza instead? Or hot fries? Come on.

He could talk to his girlfriend about the incident. Maybe find out why she was sitting next to another boy in the cafeteria, or even *if* she was sitting next to another boy in the cafeteria. He could approach the boy in a civilized manner and ask him, straight up, why he was messing with his girlfriend.

He wouldn't even have to mention the whole strawberry thing. He could hear what the dude had to say first.

My student did none of these things. Instead, he walked to the main lobby and slammed his fist through the double-plated front window. When he pulled his mangled hand back into the lobby, blood splattered everywhere. Students posted videos of the carnage online, making Jordan High School look like something out of a CSI crime scene or a bad horror movie.

This was a month before the end of the school year. My student was a senior. After vandalizing school property, he was suspended for the remainder of the semester. In addition to spending thousands of dollars on hospital bills, he wouldn't get his diploma with the rest of his classmates. Then his girlfriend broke up with him. And as far as I know, he never found out what actually happened in the cafeteria that day.

Yes, I know this is an extreme example. But all of this drama came from a rumor, and a rumor started because a group of kids wanted to stir up trouble between a boy and a girl.

For the remainder of the year, the "strawberry incident" was all that anyone wanted to talk about around school. The whole thing made me weary and sad. I find myself feeling this way more and more these days. But kids are only replicating the bad behavior of adults. No one seems to know what "entertainment" looks like anymore. We look for happiness in someone else's misery. We are like leeches, sucking pleasure from the conflict (or stupidity) of others.

Hollywood certainly makes this problem worse. Most of our movies end in a happy-ever-after because we are paying a lot of money to feel good. I like happy endings as much as the next person, but when I leave a movie theater, I want to keep talking about what I have just seen. I want to debate, to question, to wonder what will happen next. Otherwise the happy ending often feels like a sugar rush – pleasant at first but fleeting in the long run.

Take romance movies, for example. I love it when two like-minded people fall in love with each other. The world would be a better place if more of us could find someone who "completes us" or "makes us whole." But what about the years to come? Romance movies typically end at the moment when love is realized. We don't get to see the long, winding evolution of that love over time. That's because love is not always linear or inspiring, and if the statistics are correct, almost half of all marriages (not to mention all relationships) will end in failure. The world consists of real struggles, and real struggles don't always end in a happy-ever-after. Relationships can be tedious. They can be heartbreaking. They can make us lose hope in the future of humanity.

Or they can ground us in reality.

I want to be grounded in reality because I feel more alive when I have to roll up my sleeves and dig in the weeds. I love getting my face covered in sweat and grime. I love standing side by side with my wife and kids, even on the days when nothing "special" happens. Especially on the days when nothing special happens. That's when the most beautiful moments are most likely to come my way. My sons don't love me because I am some kind of incredible father-figure. They love me because they *know* me. They see me every morning when they wake up. I play with them every night, giving them baths and nagging them to brush their teeth and then reading to them right before bedtime. Their love for me stems from a slow accumulation of hours together, day after day after day. The best thing I can do for them is to be present for the daily routines of their lives.

The German philosopher Nietzsche once wrote that "One can name great men of all kinds who were very little gifted. They *acquired* greatness…they all possessed that seriousness of the efficient workman which first learns to construct the parts properly before it ventures to fashion a great whole; they allowed themselves time for it, because they took more pleasure in making the little, secondary things well than in the effect of a dazzling whole."

If we are going to serve others, whether it's the people in our community or our own family, we have to take pleasure in the little parts more than the dazzling whole.

Some of my most satisfying moments as a coach came when I was alone in the laundry room after a football game. It was usually around 10:00 on a school night. The only sound came from the whirring generator outside the open window – we never had air conditioning in the locker room, in spite of the sweat and the funk that permeated everything. I grabbed the final clean jersey and placed it into the cage. Then I locked the door and turned out the lights. I was bone tired and hadn't eaten since late morning. I probably would just crash when I got home. But before then I walked down the long hallways of the school and thought about all the noise and commotion that would fill this space in a few short hours. Nobody other than my wife knew I was here. Nobody cared, for that matter. Next week my players would put on their clean jerseys and never question how they got that way. In the morning, my first period students would expect me to teach them with the same level of enthusiasm as the day before. And I *could* do it with the same level of enthusiasm. It wasn't always easy, but when life has a purpose, we are willing to put up with almost anything.

I believe in slow-dose service. That's what teaching is all about. On the other end of the spectrum is caffeine shot service. One of my former students has made a name for himself as a traveling artist. He gets paid good money to speak at universities across the country, teaching students about the beauty of poetry and art. People leave his talks feeling inspired – kind of like a mind-blowing TED talk where an expert wins over an audience with a twenty-minute presentation about some new and exciting topic. There is a place for this kind of service, but I wonder how effective it is in the long run. We all want to be inspired. This can happen when we hear a good speaker or listen to a talented musician. But it's a caffeine shot of inspiration that inevitably fades away over time. Being present with someone day after day is so much more powerful. This is what parenting is all about, or any kind of service that grinds forward without a whole lot of regular affirmation. It is not always inspiring, but it is always important.

When my son Cason was about three years old, one of his favorite phrases was "This is the good thing…" He said it whenever he was about to launch into one of his newfound discoveries about the world. "The good thing" could be anything – the whistling sound of wind in the trees, the way my unshaven face felt against his cheeks, the smell of Saturday morning pancakes.

This is the good thing.

Serving others is most definitely a good thing. But you can't do it if you constantly need the spotlight turned on you. You've got to avoid drama. Otherwise the worst of humanity will be drawn to your light, and it will be an ugly glow, fluorescent, the kind of light that gives everything a sterile appearance.

Usually the most beautiful moments in our lives happen when we are engaged in a diligent, selfless effort towards a cause that is greater than ourselves. These moments appear when we least expect them, at any time and at any place. You can't force a beautiful moment. The magical moments in life don't happen that way. But when they do happen, they truly are a good thing.

And they are far better than any Hollywood movie.

#5

You Have to Like People

It should be a given that in order to help people, you have to like people.

But that's not always the case.

I've worked with plenty of teachers who don't like kids. Can't stand them, actually. Why, you may ask, would someone spend the bulk of their waking hours with 150 people they don't like? I don't know. I don't know why people do many of the things they do. Call it sin, karma, human frailty, or any number of other explanations. I just know that it's real.

Angry people fascinate me. They annoy me, yes, but they also fascinate me. Anger is like a weathered old tree with long, gnarly roots trailing deep beneath the surface. We don't know why the tree is dying. We just know that its leaves are withering away and its bark is rotten in several places. The problem lies in the roots, underground. We don't get to see the problem.

And so it is with people. No one enjoys being unhappy. We inflict pain on our friends and colleagues without gaining any real joy in their suffering (unless you're a sociopath, but that's a whole different story.) Anger is usually just the manifestation of something deep down, something that no one wants people to see.

As a public school teacher in a diverse city, I work with a lot of broken people. My students and their families are broken by poverty and addiction and racism and all the other -isms that plague our cities. Some of them do hateful, mean-spirited things to everyone in their path. They cut people down as a way of covering up their own pain. I see it all the time. And in my worst moments, I hate them right back. Yes, I have to admit this. I am part of a broken system that infects the hearts and souls of a community. It feeds my anger. It swallows my efforts to turn the other cheek. It festers in all of us.

For me, the first step is acknowledging that the brokenness is there. Then, and only then, can we cast it aside.

I'm not perfect. In fact, I fail most of the time. But I know brokenness when I see it. I will not let it define me.

So I'll return to that dying tree. I will care for it anyway, even when the leaves wither away and the branches sag to the ground. I will tend to it because I don't know what is happening to its roots. It's not my place to know.

It's the same way with people. You have to confront brokenness when you serve others. You also have to keep a sense of humor. Anger loves to stifle laughter. Anger loves to make us forget that the world is a joyful place full of incredible beauty.

These days I am much more willing to laugh with my students. It's not that my heart is somehow lighter – in fact, I would argue that in our current political and social divisiveness, few people are skipping through life on a bed of roses. On the contrary, I make a concerted effort to seek out happy people. They are everywhere, but for much of my life I have been too self-absorbed to notice them.

Happy people are not always bubbly people. That's just a cartoon stereotype. They are often kind of quirky.

This year I taught a kid named Nashaun. He was tall and awkward, and he had a goofy personality that got him in trouble with some of his teachers. Nashaun was the kind of kid who liked fresh food so much that he brought both the peanut butter and jelly jars to school so he could spread his sandwich right before he ate it. One day I walked into class and smelled toasted bread. I looked over and there was Nashaun in the corner of my room with a full-sized toaster, warming up his one piece of bread for the day. What possesses a teenage boy to carry around a toaster for four hours just so he can toast his one slice of bread?

Instead of rolling my eyes and beginning my lesson, I laughed. Laughter is incredibly contagious. Try watching a funny movie by yourself and then watch the same funny movie with a group of friends and you'll see the difference. We love to laugh with other people. Nashaun smiled at me. He knew what he was doing. Maybe I didn't know what he was doing, but Nashaun did.

On the last day of class, during our three-hour final exam, Nashaun hid an uncooked egg in his pocket. When the exam was over, he took out the egg, along with an old-school egg warmer that was already full of water. He was just about to plug in the egg warmer and get his water boiling when I stopped him.

This wasn't a practical joke, exactly. Nashaun didn't even seem to care if anyone saw what he was doing. That made the whole thing so much more beautiful to me. This wasn't some kind of performance. He wasn't doing this for attention. To this day I still don't know what was going on in his head, but I'm okay with that.

I need to thank Nashaun for bringing so much joy to my class. Next time I see him, I'll be sure to do just that. In previous years I would have missed the whole story. I wouldn't have even seen Nashaun for the quirky, joyful young man that he is.

How many stories like this are we missing? How many times have we failed to help someone simply because they are quiet or because another person is demanding our attention? How many times have we simply shirked our duties as humans because most of the time we feel paralyzed by the inhumanity all around us?

I believe in the power of loving other people. I believe that no community will ever feel like a sanctuary unless we can break down the barriers that separate us. We can talk all we want about the obstacles on the surface, because ugliness will always be there if we keep our eyes focused upon it. We have to go deep. It's the only way.

Here's what it is like to go beneath the surface:

Our older son Brett was due to be born in about two weeks. It was late-summer, right before school was about to start back. I was already in the middle of two-a-day football practices. Jenni was so pregnant that she could barely move, but she still had to drive to work every day. For all of these reasons, I was about as distracted as I have ever been in my life. What kind of a father was I going to be? How were we going to make this work financially? Would my marriage to Jenni ever be the same after this, with no sleep and a baby who needed every waking moment of our attention?

Yes, I was stressed.

The grass in our yard was getting long, so I decided to cut it on a Sunday afternoon. I did it fast, almost running behind my lawnmower as my brain swam with all of these unsettling questions. I made a turn next to my neighbor Elias's yard and carefully pivoted beside his bed of straw. Elias was standing next to his mailbox. I waved to him as I finished my loop.

Elias waved to me as I finished the front yard. I ran over to shake his hand quickly and then get back to my work. For all I knew, Jenni could be going into labor at any moment.

I knew something was wrong when Elias wouldn't shake my hand. "Stu, you need to watch where you're stepping. That's my flower bed. I don't appreciate you doing that."

"Excuse me?" I said, confused.

"My flower bed," Elias continued, glaring at me. "You stepped in my flowerbed on purpose, didn't you?"

I stared at Elias and wiped the sweat from my forehead. *What the hell was going on here?*

Elias is a very private man, but never in the five years of living next door had we exchanged an unkind word to each other. Elias played football in high school, and we liked to talk sports. It was our common bond, something that linked us together even though we came from different generations and his skin happened to be darker than mine.

I felt the anger rising to my face. I'd always tried to be considerate of his property. I always took the time to exchange pleasantries with him. Where was this coming from?

I thought about lashing out. What right did Elias have to yell at me like this? I had enough to worry about right now.

But I lowered my eyes instead. "I'm sorry, Elias," I said. "I didn't mean to insult you."

Elias sighed and then stared off into the distance. "No," he said. "It's not you."

We stood there for a minute in silence, and then Elias looked at me again. "I was out walking with Sheryl the other night – same route we've been taking for the past twenty years – when this old white dude walks past me on the street. He looked no different from any old white dude you might see. Then he glances over his shoulder and says, 'Apes like you need to go back with your own kind.' Then he kept right on walking. Never seen the man before in my life. I just stood there, didn't say a damn thing to him as he walked away. Not a damn thing."

I stood next to Elias and did the only thing I could think of. I raised my eyes from the ground and refused to look away. I watched the pain hover on his face and then slowly disappear, as if he had practiced this routine time and time again. We stood there for a while, not saying anything, just letting the silence fill the space between us.

What could I possibly say to Elias?

I'm sorry. I get what you are going through.

But I couldn't say that. I had no idea what he was going through, what he had dealt with for years and years. I could dismiss the man who insulted Elias as a bigot, someone different from me, someone on the margins who had nothing in common with me except our skin color. That would be easier. I could feel better about myself that way.

Or I could try to see Elias and let him see me, eye to eye, two people stuck in the muck of a broken world, trying to find a better way forward.

Elias is still my neighbor, and that uncomfortable conversation lingers at the edges of our friendship. I'm sure I feel it in a different way than he does. After all, I am white and he is black. But I trust him in a way that was never possible before we opened up to each other, and I hope that he trusts me too.

On that sweltering summer day seven years ago, I saw beneath the surface of my neighbor. Elias and I chose to do something painful and to face this pain in an open way. We took a difficult step together.

The world is full of atoms moving randomly inside of our bodies and bouncing from one person to another, connecting us in a web, repelling us sometimes, getting things confused. We have a moral responsibility to see people for who they are and, more importantly, for who they can become. We have to believe that we are more than just atoms randomly bouncing through the air. We are so much more.

If we don't consider our neighbor with openness, if we don't see the delightful things people do when no one is looking, how will we ever be more than specks of dust on the bottom of someone's shoes? We will be nothing. We *are* nothing.

But it doesn't have to be this way. We can be better than this.

#6

Hard Work

Life can be a grind sometimes. We wake up, go to work, go home, fall to sleep, and do it all over again, just waiting for Friday night to arrive so we can finally be free.

But what does it mean to be free? I have to ask myself this question from time to time because it feels like the world owns us for much of our waking hours.

Just get to the weekend. Just earn that money. Just pay those bills. Just grind it out and wait for the next vacation or the beer at the end of the day or whatever else we do to feel something, anything.

I recognize this. I see this. But I fall victim to it anyway

In 17 years I've gotten up before 5:15 a.m. over 2,720 times. I take the same five mile drive to work past the same houses and the same people walking their dogs. I park in the same spot in the school parking lot, open the same classroom door, room 413, then wait for the same bell to start the day. Teenagers are always tired first period. I never see the sun over the mobile trailer roofs until about noon. It's a never-ending cycle. After work I go home and step into parent mode.

How many hundreds of diapers have I changed? How many bath times with my boys, followed by story time and a good-night kiss on the forehead? Night time blends into morning, then night time again.

The grind is ugly, but it is also quite beautiful if you look at it more closely.

I am not a sentimental teacher. I am not moved easily, and I don't go looking for the kind of Hollywood moments that we expect to find in a fulfilling career.

But one scenario always gets me: I love to watch a person change over time. I love to watch them show up day after day, letting their courage shine through in their willingness to keep showing up, even when most people would have given up long ago.

There is something sacred about showing up. A few years ago I traveled around North Carolina interviewing high school football coaches who have made a positive impact on their communities. I traveled from the Cherokee reservation deep in the Appalachian Mountains all the way to the coast, spending time in both rural and urban communities. Some of these places were thriving and some of them appeared to be stuck in the past. Along the way I realized that most of these coaches were average men, and none of them were doing anything revolutionary with their football programs. The key, I learned, was that they showed up year after year. People knew them. They entrusted their sons to play for them. The naysayers realized that these coaches weren't leaving anytime soon, so they might as well get with the program.

Presence can be the most powerful tool in a servant's toolbox.

As a new dad I've been thinking a lot about my own happy childhood. What can I learn from the way my parents raised me? I look at them now, as they get older and I take on more of the caregiving role, and I wonder what made me feel so secure as a child. My parents made plenty of mistakes back then. They weren't perfect. But they were consistent. They established clear routines, and I knew exactly what to expect from one day to the next.

This trait is one of the hallmarks of my classroom these days. I am obsessively organized. I do the same things at the same time every class period. My students eventually make fun of me for it, but there's always a little bit of respect beneath the teasing. They like the routines. They want to know what's going to happen next. Once a kid is comfortable in their environment, they will start taking risks and not even realize they are doing it.

Trust is one of the most important components of serving others. We have to show up day after day after day. I can't say this enough. It has to feel repetitive and almost comical in its regularity. I came into class a few weeks back and one of my students literally groaned in my face. "Mr. Albright, when are you *ever* going to get sick?" We all laughed, even though there was some truth in his complaint. He was tired of seeing me every single day. He didn't want to do any work. But we were able to laugh about it because, beneath the groan, he was expressing a deep-seated appreciation (or at least respect) for my willingness to show up so dependably. It's the kind of thing we tend to appreciate long after the fact but rarely in the moment.

Think back to your own childhood, to the times when you felt most vulnerable or most alone. Stability matters in these moments. Predictability can be priceless. We count on our parents and teachers and community leaders to guide us with a steady hand.

Growing up, I knew exactly what to expect on Friday nights in the fall. My father would come home from a long day at work, pick me up, and we would drive to a high school football game. We got there an hour early, sat in the same seats, ordered the same pre-game meal of hot dogs covered in chili. Then we would talk about our highs and lows from the week as we watched the two teams warm up. Everything in my life felt upside down in so many ways, but those Friday nights were predictable. They were sacred. I cherished these moments high above the football field, the sounds and the smells and the crisp feel of autumn overtaking summer, knowing that my dad was there to protect me and to comfort me with these routines, letting me relax to the point where I could appreciate the beauty around me. I could finally think outside of my own head.

I'm sure it was hard for my dad to leave work sometimes, but he always did. He was patient. He always listened to me. He recognized the importance of these routines, so simple but also so life-changing.

Showing up and working hard are important character traits. A growing body of research is starting to show us just how important these character traits can be.

For years the most common predictor of life success was our intelligence. I remember being a kid and asking my mom what my IQ score was. She refused to tell me, and it used to drive me crazy. Today I am glad that I never knew my score. A high IQ would have nudged me to be lazy, complacent, and entitled. A low score would have crushed me. I was hard enough on myself as it was; the last thing I needed was a number telling me that I wasn't good enough. Who knows what my score was. I'll never know. I never *want* to know.

Unfortunately, IQ scores and high GPAs are not always a good predictor of success in college and then later in life. Experts in the field of psychology have wrestled with this dilemma for years. In 2004, researchers Christopher Peterson and Martin E. P. Seligman published an influential book on the science of character called *Character Strengths and Virtues: a Handbook and Classification*. The book exhaustively collected a list of virtues that were universally accepted in all societies throughout time. "Virtues," they wrote, "are much more interesting than laws." People follow laws out of obedience to a higher authority. But a virtue, or character trait, could be developed over time if someone could just understand the practical value of character in their life.

Over the years, Peterson and Seligman narrowed their list of 24 virtues down to seven traits that were most likely to predict high achievement and overall life satisfaction. The list included grit, self-control, zest, social intelligence, gratitude, optimism, and curiosity.

Enter Angela Duckworth. She cut her teeth working under Seligman in the Psychology Department at the University of Pennsylvania. A former teacher, Duckworth was fascinated by the disconnect between test scores in school and high achievement later in life. She knew that childhood trauma played a role. Kids who experience instability in their childhood go through a lot of stress. This stress wreaks havoc on their brains and leads to all kinds of physical and psychological ailments later in life. On the flip side, Duckworth had worked with plenty of brilliant Ivy League students who had never really struggled before. She called these students "the fragile perfects," because the moment they hit their first real road block, they folded under the pressure.

Duckworth studied her mentor's list of seven virtues and concluded that grit was perhaps the best predictor of life success.

"The scientific research is very clear that experiencing trauma without control can be debilitating," Duckworth writes. "But I also worry about people who cruise through life, friction-free, for a long, long time before encountering their first real failure. They have so little practice falling and getting up again. They have so many reasons to stick with a fixed mindset."

Grit is all about follow-through, about doing the kind of dirty work that doesn't bring immediate results.

Duckworth started testing her theories about grit on students ranging from elementary school all the way to the military academies. The results were both startling and consistent.

In one representative study she found that "Teachers who, in college, had demonstrated productive follow-through in a few extracurricular commitments were more likely to stay in teaching and, furthermore, were more effective in producing academic gains in their students. In contrast, persistence and effectiveness in teaching had absolutely no measurable relationship with teachers' SAT scores, their college GPAs, or interview ratings of their leadership potential."

Duckworth's bestselling book *Grit: The Power of Passion and Perseverance* has shaken up the debate about student achievement. Character, Duckworth argues, can be taught to anyone, while IQ is a fixed product of genetics, wealth, and privilege. Character could be our best way to level the playing field between the haves and the have-nots.

While reading *Grit*, I immediately thought about why I loved coaching football. I've been able to track my former players later into adulthood, and, as a whole, they have greater success than my non-athletic students (or at least my students who were not deeply immersed in some kind of extracurricular activity.) During practice, we often created situations in which our players had to overcome adversity. Most coaches make the mistake of leaving their conditioning period (usually sprints or "gassers") to the end of practice. Kids know these sprints are coming and they save up just enough energy to get through them. What we did instead was to interrupt practice at random, unexpected moments to put our players through sprints. Then we immediately jumped right back into working on our offense or defense. We wanted to see how our guys reacted under stress. Would they be able to think clearly, or would they get distracted and turn on each other? We wanted them ready so that when the lights went up on Friday night, they were prepared for adversity. The key to all of this was control. We never did these practice techniques to punish guys, and we never pushed them over the edge of what they could handle. But we wanted to nudge them closer to the edge than they were comfortable.

I firmly believe that grit matters. It made me a better football player in high school, a better student in college, and a better teacher throughout my career.

The character movement focuses on the kind of traits that will lead to a successful life. It's worth pointing out that happiness is a subjective term. Running makes me happy, but for many people, running a mile feels like torture. I hate heavy metal music, but Metallica may bring you to enlightenment. Human interests are incredibly complex.

Happiness can be defined in many different ways. Joy, on the other hand, is much more universal.

Happiness comes from external sources. Joy comes from within. And there's no greater way to feel joy than by serving others.

I try (and often fail) to embody the seven character traits that Seligman created. But lately I've been thinking about character in a new way. When most people think about virtues like grit or social intelligence or curiosity, we naturally look at them through a very narrow, individual lens. *How can grit lead me to a higher paying job? Will increased social intelligence allow me to make more friends? How can curiosity open up doors in my personal and professional life?*

Like so much of human nature, our focus inevitably turns to the Self. But what if we saw grit as a way to serve others more effectively? What if we saw the daily grind as something sacred, something to make the world a better place?

I love the way Henry David Thoreau speaks about simplicity: "If one advances confidently in the direction of his dreams," Thoreau writes, "and endeavors to live the life which he has imagined, he will meet with a success unexpected in common hours … In proportion as he simplifies his life, the laws of the universe will appear less complex, and solitude will not be solitude, nor poverty, nor weakness. If you have built castles in the air, your work need not be lost; that is where they should be. Now put the foundations under them."

Simplicity and grit have a lot in common. We all need order in our lives. Otherwise we find ourselves caught up in the chaos of technological change, political strife, and a society that encourages us to put our self-interests first. Sometimes we need to let our mind run free. We need to block out the noise and go to work.

I used to think that older adults enjoyed gardening because it was slow-paced and easy to do. Gardening was a way for our society to give the elderly some fresh air and to keep them physically active. Kind of like bingo with a little vitamin D added for good measure. Now I know better. We don't give senior citizens enough credit for their lifetime of accumulated wisdom. There's a reason why gardening is such a powerful metaphor. A gardener tills the soil and carefully plants different kinds of seeds. She trusts the process, knowing that a little green seed will one day grow into something beautiful. Weeds will appear along the way, and the gardener will get her hands dirty as she clears them out one by one. The sun will be hot on her neck. Her back will ache from bending over. The work will feel tedious at first. There will be no immediate results. Some people will say that the magic happens when a tiny seed grows into a flowering plant. I think the magic happens while we pull the weeds and do the dirty work that no one notices.

These days I watch older adults and imagine their silence not as a way of receding from the world but as a way of finally understanding their place in it. They live with a sense of clarity that eludes so many of us. We should watch how they go about their days, rarely drawing attention to themselves, seeing a world full of treasures that are hidden in plain sight.

Gardening is a perfect metaphor when it comes to service. No one plants a seed and expects it to grow overnight. The gardener toils with aching hands in the dirt, knowing that patience is essential. They work really hard with nothing to show for their efforts – at least not yet. The ground is still covered in dirt.

But they don't see an empty field. They see the possibilities yet to come, the green stems and the birdsong and the sweet smells of new life. They toil now in order to reap the rewards later. Sometimes much, much later.

I believe in hard work. I believe in showing up every day, even when no one sees you grinding it out. Especially when no one sees you grinding it out. That's when service becomes all the more sacred.

#7
Living in the Here and Now

For a decade or so of my adult life, I spent my summers writing and coaching. I got up early and worked on my latest book project or meetings for about six hours before heading to football practice. Sometimes the words flowed easily. Other times they did not. But I always showed up at my desk and let the creative process play out. Some kind of new idea usually came to the surface.

After a long day of deep thinking, I was always ready to get outside in the heat and coach football for the rest of the afternoon. I could run around and yell and be part of the world again. The heat never bothered me – this was my kind of gardening, with sweat soaking my clothes as I coached my wide receivers. The time flew by because I was completely immersed in something worthwhile.

I enjoyed this schedule – folding into myself in the morning, folding outwards for the rest of the day. Work never felt like work. Time passed by pleasantly.

Before I knew it, I was no longer 22 years old. I was pushing 40, with a wife and two young kids. I was able to keep up my writing/coaching routine after Brett and Cason were born because my wife is a saint. She made the sacrifice to stay home with the kids after they were born. She believed in what I was doing. She put her career on hold so that I could write and coach. And when I got home late at night, she ate dinner with me well after 9 p.m.

Summers were hard for Jenni. While I was feeding my mind with writing and my spirit with coaching, she was doing the daily, repetitive tasks of feeding our boys, coming up with new games to play with them, letting them tug on her with constant questions and demands.

Jenni has this incredible way of living in the moment. When she smiles, her whole face lights up. It's the kind of little detail that all men should look for in a wife. Every part of her is full of joy. When she gets frustrated and tired, the joy is still there. She is always alive, heart and soul. Brett and Cason are lucky to have her as their mother.

I don't have many regrets in my adult life. I'm proud of the books I wrote during those 16 summers. Writing has given me a platform to speak about public education to civic leaders across the state. I'm also proud of the relationships I've built with so many young men on the football field. Those relationships didn't end when my players graduated. They continue to be a vital part of my life and my commitment to service.

But I do have one regret.

I've tried to live a good life, to live in the present, and to use my talents to benefit other people. For the most part I have done this pretty well. And I think I've done these things for the right reasons. But life is a balancing act. Even the noblest act of service needs to be done with the understanding that life is finite. We have a limited set of resources. There are only so many hours in a day. I don't regret the thousands of hours I devoted to coaching. What I do regret is the perspective I brought to this work. I saw coaching as the ultimate way for me to serve. I tried to be a good husband and a good father, but I sometimes lost sight of the most important kind of service of all: how we treat those who are closest to our hearts.

This past summer my wife and I switched roles. She started a new job, so my mornings of uninterrupted writing were gone. I'm typing this book late at night as my eyes grow heavy. I write for an hour or two and then fall into bed. It will probably take me years to finish this project.

That's fine. Here's what I get to do instead: I get to spend all day, every day, with my two sons. We call it Camp Albright. My boys and I take hikes in the morning. We play card games and read books together. Brett and Cason push each other's buttons, and a good day means that no punches have been thrown. I don't feel like a very good parent sometimes. I don't go through these days joyfully soaking up every moment. But I laugh a lot more. I get to spend long, uninterrupted days with my sons. I get to answer (or try to answer) their constant questions about life. I get to see how big the world appears to a child.

Ralph Waldo Emerson once wrote, "To speak truly, few adult persons can see nature. Most persons do not see the sun. At least they have a very superficial seeing. The sun illuminates only the eye of the man, but shines into the eye and the heart of the child. The lover of nature is he whose inward and outward senses are still truly adjusted to each other; who has retained the spirit of infancy even into the era of manhood."

I agree with Emerson. Children experience the world with their head and their hearts, while most adults lose the ability to see the world with their hearts. Unfortunately, that's where joy often exists.

This new summer routine has allowed me to see the world with my heart again. I've tried to be fully present with my children. I've tried to see parenting as the greatest form of service I can offer to the world. The world needs teachers, coaches, and mentors. The world also needs children who grow up with their parents close by their side.

I know that most parents don't get to spend this much time with their kids. I'm lucky to have a job with such a long window of open time and the financial resources to make it happen. But my point is larger than this. I want to be present in the world in both large and small ways. I've lived a rich, public life, but I've been so focused on serving my community that I've forgotten how important it is to serve my family with the same amount of urgency.

I'm trying to change that now. Every day I spend with my boys is a treasure. Every conversation over coffee with my wife is a sacred act. Every day that I wake up is a reason to give thanks.

My favorite Pixar movie of all time is *Up*. If you haven't seen this movie yet, go watch it with your kids, your grandparents, basically anyone who cares about what it means to be human. *Up* is about an old man named Carl who is mourning the loss of his wife Ellie. Carl and Ellie always planned to take a big adventure together before they died. They would travel to South America and build their dream home next to a majestic waterfall. Then their life would be complete.

Ellie dies before they can take this adventure.

After Ellie's death, Carl finds a scrapbook that his wife made when she was a little girl. *My Adventure Book*, she called it. The scrapbook is filled with pictures of her dreams cobbled together in drawings and newspaper clippings. In the middle of the scrapbook is a page titled "Stuff I'm Going to Do." Carl always thought that the rest of the scrapbook was empty. What did their marriage add up to, after all? Every time they saved up money for their big adventure, something always came up. Some unexpected expense, a broken leg, the trauma of a miscarriage – the very real obstacles that always seem to get in the way of actually living. But just as Carl is about to close the book, he is shocked to find page after page filled with pictures of their life together. All the little adventures that any of us can relate to. A wedding photo. Feeding pigeons in the park. Drinking coffee together at breakfast. His wife staring out a window with a peaceful look on her face.

These were the real adventures. These were the moments that defined a life well-lived.

I challenge anyone to watch this scene without crying. It speaks to our longing for peace in a world filled with unreasonable expectations, a world that tells us that happiness is just around the corner.

But happiness is right here, right now with the people who know us best.

Joy can be here as well. And joy brings the kind of lasting peace that never grows old.

#8

Long-range Thinking

I'm trying to live in the here and now. I'm trying to enjoy every moment. Camp Albright is coming to an end. A new school year is just around the corner, and I hope that I can do a better job of being present. We'll see how it goes.

The here and now is beautiful, but it can also be ugly. It's easy to live in a constant state of negativity. As humans, this seems to be our default setting. Being optimistic requires work, patience, and long-range thinking.

I recently took a trip to the Blue Ridge Mountains with my wife. It was a quick, one-night stay, but we got in plenty of hiking and good conversations while our boys spent time with Jenni's parents. As we drove back to civilization the next morning, I remember wondering if I would ever have another relaxing day like this again. Sure, the odds are pretty good that I'll get to see a beautiful sunset in the coming weeks, or have a good meal with my wife. These are normal, everyday things that happen to most of us on a regular basis. But a tiny part of me still wondered if that was too much to ask for. What right did I have to *expect* moments of peace? I could be dead in the morning. I could lose my job. Our country could become entangled in the next world war.

This isn't rational. I know that. But my brain isn't rational most of the time. I rarely enjoy the here and now because I am always pre-occupied with the future, and I can't look forward to the future because I am stuck in the day to day worries that, while fleeting, have a way of derailing me from living in service to my family and to my community.

So if I'm going to serve others, it's not enough to live in the here and now. I also need to see the long game. I need to enjoy the beautiful sunset right before me, and then I need to imagine the beautiful sunsets still to come. They will be there in the future. I have to keep telling ourselves that they will be there.

I try to see the best in people. This doesn't always work, especially when I get near the end of a busy semester and I cannot tolerate one more whining complaint or catch one more student plagiarizing an essay (as savvy as teenagers are about technology, they seem to forget that a google search will catch just about anything.)

It's easy to get consumed by anger, and I'm as guilty as the next person.

"Of the Seven Deadly Sins," Frederick Buechner writes, "anger is possibly the most fun. To lick your wounds, to smack your lips over grievances long past, to roll over your tongue the prospect of bitter confrontations still to come, to savor to the last toothsome morsel both the pain you are given and the pain you are giving back – in many ways it is a feast fit for a king. The chief drawback is that what you are wolfing down is yourself. The skeleton at the feast is you."

Yes, I have eaten this meal before. And yes, it has consumed me.

But these days, even in my lowest moments, I try to see the best in people.

This has become much easier in recent years. My students grow up and then come back to visit me as adults. Often they are very different from the kids I once taught. They are less bitter, slower to judge, quicker to say a kind word. I try to remember this when a difficult student walks into my room. They will not always be like this. After all, it's not about me. It's not about me. It's not about me...

A few years ago, I decided to take a closer look at why some of my students rush headlong into their adult years, while others seem to drift without purpose or direction. Instead of grappling with this issue on a macro scale, I did a deep dive into the lives of two of my former students: George and Siddiq. I believe in the power of stories, and while statistical data is important, stories bring an issue to life in a way that numbers never can.

Over a three-year period, I spent countless hours interviewing these two former students about their experiences in high school, both inside my classroom and throughout their daily lives. I wanted to know about every one of their successes, their failures, the moments when they felt hopeless, as well as the moments when they decided who they wanted to become as an adult.

George is the son of Japanese immigrants who run a sushi restaurant here in Durham. He constantly clashed with his parents over his behavior in school, and his father once beat him so badly that George was placed into foster care. At age 15, George sold weed to half of my high school until he was kicked out for the remainder of the school year. Lonely and depressed, he discovered spoken word poetry. When George returned to my high school the following year, he started a poetry club and began his ascension to the top of the poetry world, eventually traveling around the country and winning competitions against professional poets twice his age.

Siddiq was always the biggest guy in his class. He was also a ticking time bomb, bottling up his anger while his parents fought in the bedroom next door. Football became his outlet, but it wasn't enough. When some of his friends joined a gang, he joined too. It wasn't long before Siddiq had to decide between his football teammates and his fellow gang members. One night, after almost getting caught up in a shooting at a party, Siddiq decided to leave his gang life behind. He eventually used his athletic ability to earn a spot on the University of Delaware football team. At Delaware, Siddiq became a star on the football field, and his passion for community service led newspapers to call him "the Gandhi of Delaware."

As George and Siddiq's high school English teacher, I watched their lives unfold at a critical stage of their development. Their stories illustrate the major obstacles that students face in a public school, such as poverty, broken families, identity issues, racism, and the daunting challenge of finding a purpose in the larger world.

George and Siddiq discovered their purpose. They found something to be passionate about in high school. For George it was poetry. For Siddiq it was football. For both of them it was storytelling. These passions pushed George and Siddiq to do well in school. And the more they pursued their passions, the more they were propelled into the outside world. They moved beyond their comfort zone, beyond their narrow view of the far horizon, meeting new people and learning to see themselves in new ways.

The beautiful thing about discovering your own story is that it compels you to be interested in the lives of other people. You develop empathy, and if enough young people could learn how to develop empathy, the world would be a much better place.

I like to think that I played a small role in the journeys of George and Siddiq. Maybe I did, maybe I didn't. They certainly deserve most of the credit. I am in awe of their bravery and their willingness to fall down and to get back up again.

I thought I knew these guys pretty well when they were in my class, but I underestimated them. I couldn't see where they would end up. Unfortunately, I do this all the time, judging people for who they are (or who I think they are) instead of who they will become.

Spending time with George and Siddiq got me thinking about my other former students. I'd just resigned from coaching, and I was on the fence about my teaching job. The wound was still fresh. I was in a reflective mood.

What were the rest of my students up to? I wondered. I'd taught thousands of teenagers over the years, and while I managed to stay in touch with a number of them, I still wondered if my work had made any kind of difference. I know that sounds melodramatic. But when you are tired and burned out and a little bit sad, all the artificiality gets stripped away and you really do wonder if anything really matters.

So I began to reach out to my former students. I used Facebook and LinkedIn and old email addresses, not knowing what kind of response I would get. I wondered how their lives had changed since high school. What were they most proud of? What had been their biggest frustrations? How had writing helped them in the adult world?

I felt like I was shouting down from a mountaintop into a densely-wooded valley. Was anyone listening? Would my words simply echo back up to me in the wind, empty and hollow? That's how I was feeling at the time – empty and hollow – so I half-expected nothing in return.

I'm happy to say that I was wrong.

Emails started to pour in from students I hadn't heard from in years. Some had just entered the working world after college. Others were married with kids and pushing 30 years old. Some were still living in Durham. Others had moved to far-away places like New York, California, Ireland, and even China. They were doctors and teachers, Olympic athletes and award-winning journalists. Some of them had really struggled after high school. Others hadn't written much of anything since our class. But all of them were open and honest about their successes and failures.

Their words filled me up again. They reminded me that the world is full of so much goodness, so much to be grateful for. Most people really do want to make the world a better place. Our successes come in different forms. Our lives move forward in fits and starts, the ending uncertain and a little bit scary. Sometimes our dreams go unrealized. Sometimes we find happiness and joy in the most unexpected places.

I got 51 lengthy responses from my former students, enough to fill an entire book. Here in a condensed form are two of the most memorable responses:

***

Alaina

I, like many high school students, went to college straight out of high school. I decided to go to UNC Chapel Hill because I had been told that it had a good creative writing program, and by the end of high school, writing was the only thing I seemed to be any good at.

But when I arrived at UNC as a freshman I was lost. I think most people are lost when they first get to college. I guess the difference is I never ended up finding my way, or finding this "niche" that I hear people speak of.

I took a spattering of different classes my first year, searching for something enlightening or expansive. Instead, mostly what I found were people who seemed to me so far removed from the world that I lived in that I couldn't contextualize hardly any of what they had to say. Why was it important that I knew about Kant and his ethics? Why was everyone so obsessed with books that old, dead white guys had written? In all honesty though, I missed a lot of these classes because I spent my first semester in love with a rich boy from Florida. Through him I got lost in a whirl of drugs and music, and nights spent lying on the floor in the dark listening to side B of Pink Floyd's Meddle and feeling untethered and unsure. I was basically the biggest cliché ever, but I drank a lot of black coffee and thought I was really onto something here.

But I wasn't. Spring came. I stopped doing drugs. I went on runs and started eating again. Summer came and went and I don't remember much of it because nothing great ever results from staying home in the summer. Classes started again in the Fall, and one sunny afternoon, over a book about the John Robert's Court, I realized how profoundly, deeply unhappy I had become despite my best efforts to "make the most of things."

So I dropped out of school after my first semester of sophomore year. I started working at a fancy restaurant to save money. I learned a lot about wine and about the world of working people. I also learned about poverty, and struggle. I worked and saved. I didn't know exactly what I was saving for, but I knew that money was freedom. Slowly, and then quickly, Spring started to bloom and I decided I wanted to go work in Yellowstone National Park as a maid. I had never left the East Coast, and in April I boarded a United flight to Bozeman, Montana. I can't explain what happened. I don't understand it entirely, but when I landed in Montana I felt like I had finally found what I had been looking for. Finally, I had found where I was supposed to be. Here was the space I had been looking for! Here was the room I needed to breathe and stretch out and see for what seemed like forever. The West felt instantly familiar and freeing in a way that nothing in my whole life ever had. Still, when I think about the first time I saw Montana, I get chills.

Working in Yellowstone National Park was strange and beautiful and very sad. It was in Yellowstone that I first made contact with a social species of people that I'd never encountered before: drifters, professional wanderers, vagabonds, park-hoppers, psycho-spiritual masqueraders, addicts, thieves — rootless people with lots of stories and few prospects. It was the first time I realized that there were people living life differently, and that was intriguing to me. For a while I thought I could be one of them— live out of a suitcase and see the world. I read *On The Road* by Jack Kerouac and *The Electric Kool-Aid Acid Test.* I practiced hitchhiking on endless, open western roads. I ate mushrooms. I got into some eastern philosophy stuff. I got my first tattoo. I listened to a lot of The Grateful Dead. I explored vast portions of Yellowstone Park and the Grand Tetons.

I cultivated stories and experiences, but I started to become suspicious of the weightlessness of this rootless life. After about a month in the park I started to fall into a deep and debilitating depression. I do not know how to describe the sadness I felt. All I can say is that I stopped feeling like a person. Instead of the stone, I felt like the ripple. I cried most days by a large river that ran through the park. And every day, by this river, on a rock, I wrote. I had no friends here among the drifters and the van-dwellers. I was alone, except for the books that I had brought with me and the notebook that I wrote in every day. I chronicled everything. And finally when I started taking medicine, and my world lightened, I chronicled my healing. But still, as the season drew to a close and others around me began making arrangements to go to Asia for the winter, or work at ski resorts in Colorado, I bought a ticket back home.

When I got back to North Carolina, I again started working. I wasn't yet ready to relinquish what I then thought of as my "freedom" by going back to school, which seemed even more cloistering now that I had experienced the grand space of the big western sky. I decided I was going to hike the Pacific Crest Trail (PCT.) The PCT is a 2,600-mile foot path that goes from the Mexican border in Southern California, up to the Canadian border in Northern Washington. I worked and saved up money, researched and trained. And then in April 2016, I flew out to San Diego to start this six-month long hike. On April 4th, I stood at the California-Mexican border…and started walking. Here is some advice: if you wait until you are ready, you will never do anything. Here is some other advice: you are more capable than you can ever imagine.

I hiked a little over 1,600 miles. I got to the border of California and Oregon, and due to some health issues had to come home. It is very difficult to describe what it is like to be hiking for five months straight. It is impossible to convey the bone crunching weight of a backpack filled with a week and a half worth of food. It is impossible to explain what happens to the body when you run out of water in the Mojave Desert. I cannot adequately describe the physical pain of bloody skin peeling off heels, the moment your foot almost lands on a rattle snake, or the split second that you lose your balance on an icy mountain pass. I also cannot describe the love, compassion and beauty that I was so humbled by during these five months. I am not a religious person, but during my time on the Pacific Crest Trail, I think I understood more what people mean by God. At least I know what God means to me. Throughout these five months I wrote every single day. I have four journals with the dust of the western wind still in their pages, dried out by the desert air. I have only one regret from my time on the trail. I regret that I was not able to capture and preserve with words what it was I felt during this time. Words have literally saved my life, given me meaning, provided me with a friend, a purpose, a guide. In many ways, they have been the connecting thread of my life, from the time I was four years old dictating stories to my mother, up until now, as I write this. Yet I regret that my words are not enough to capture what can only be felt and remembered with the soul.

In the Spring of 2017 I finally decided to come back to UNC. Returning to school was difficult. There are trade-offs you make when you uproot yourself, when you create your own plan. I am alone here now at school. The friends I had before are gone. I have a lifetime's worth of experience, but my day to day life is quite isolated. Fortunately, I have a lot of practice with being alone, so it doesn't bother me that much.

I am 22 now. I feel like an adult. I have credit. I know how to sign leases. I check e-mail regularly. I know a lot about health insurance and taxes. But what really makes me an adult is the fact that I am independent—not just financially, but emotionally. If I read through my life's writing, from the time that I was a little girl up until now, something emerges: I read myself growing up. I have an account of how I have chosen to craft my life and my person. I can read, on paper, in my own hand writing, the evolution of my mind and my heart. Through the process of becoming myself, which was often a messy, scary process, writing has been my mooring. I am not sure what exactly I am proud of, and what was difficult, because everything I am proud of was difficult. And I think that is important. Often, the hardest things in life are the things from which we gain most. But I truly believe you can do most anything, if you dare.

***

Alaina recently moved to Colorado to get her MFA degree in creative writing. Before long, she will get to serve others through the act of teaching. I look forward to following her along this journey. As you can see, Alaina is a phenomenal writer – one of the two strongest writers I have ever taught.

The other writer you are about to meet is Emily. Emily has always been fascinated by Manhattan. She even wrote a novel about the city when she was a senior in my high school creative writing class. Back then, Emily explored this unfamiliar place through the world of fiction; now she lives in New York full time as an adult. Here's what she had to say about her transition into adulthood:

***

Emily

I wrote daily throughout my senior year in college, but after graduation I slipped from fiction, focusing almost completely on my reporting. I had been living in New York for a year and had graduated from an investigative reporting program at Columbia University. I had no job, no prospects and an impossibly high rent. I hadn't written a single word of fiction in a year.

I ran quickly through my savings, alternating my days between applying for jobs, watching *telenovelas* and drinking whisky by three in the afternoon. Once, I went to the store to buy a jug of juice and my $3.65 purchase was rejected on my debit card, my credit card and every other card I had in my wallet. I ran them all through twice even though I knew I had no money. I returned home empty-handed and went to my writing desk (covered over with books and magazines) to fish through my drawer for change. I returned to the store, buying the juice in quarters, nickels and dimes.

A few weeks later, miserable in a listless routine, I decided to write a short story based on a series of photographs. I wrote every day for a week, while applying to several more jobs. A few weeks later, I received two job offers on the same day; I took the one at *The New York Times*.

But on the day I got the call with the job offer, I got another call: this one from my parents. I had just ordered an ice cream cone, and I answered as I walked back to my apartment in the summer heat, my phone pressed between my ear and my shoulder.

"Do you have a minute?" my mother asked when I answered, and her voice sounded strange and different, as though boiled down and rung through a strainer.

She had been diagnosed with breast cancer, she told me, and she would start treatment in the next few weeks. I stopped walking. The ice cream dripped down my hand in pink raspberry rivulets. I asked about the prognosis, how far the cancer had gone, when treatment would start, what the treatment would be. The next year would be spent asking much the same questions.

As an only child with no family above the Mason-Dixon line, I felt very much alone in New York. I had just started work and had little ability or money to take time off to fly home. I received all my news over phone and text, worrying from afar and pouring myself into my reporting, staying at the office until 2:00 a.m. just to avoid returning to an empty apartment. When I would finally go to bed, I played rap music at full volume to keep out the silence and slept fitfully.

Even in the months after my mother's recovery, the guilt her cancer brought, along with the helplessness and loneliness I'd felt in the past year lingered. And as I struggled with work and disappointments in love and friendship, I felt the darkness of those summer months from my first year creeping in. More than once, I awoke sprawled facedown on my floor, too exhausted or drunk or careless to make it to my bed.

What finally brought me back – first to a better disposition and then to a better outlook on relationships and work – was once again turning to the written word. (I had fallen out of the writing habit, shortly after my mother's diagnosis.) After late nights reporting on the crime beat, I'd return home, only able to sleep after writing short snippets of fiction. I wrote without intention – not bothering to title the work for the first 50,000 words – and unsure of what it was or could be until finally handing it over to a friend from a college workshopping class. I now call the novel – about a crime reporter in her third year living in New York City – a highly fictionalized version of my same year.

But the real healing came long before the book had taken shape; it came in those first few sentences blinking back at me in an untitled Word document. When I finally started the book, I hadn't written seriously in more than two years, and writing anything other than fact came with difficulty; writing about myself was even harder. Throughout my years of writing fiction, I'd always steered clear of my own struggles and insecurities, writing characters I aspired to become and would never actually be.

But this time, in order to write, I knew I had to do it differently. I thought back to my first creative writing classes in high school. I imagined myself back in Mr. Albright's classroom – the walls covered in book covers, a poster with the misspelled GENIOUS in bright neon colors above his computer. I remembered the feel of my desk, the excitement as people passed stories down the rows, the deep dark truths revealed on those pages. I checked in with some of those people in my first creative writing class – saw how far they'd come, how much happier they were – and decided that this time I'd write my own dark truth.

And remembering the way we had all read each other's work and learned about each other's lives, without judgment or condemnation, I forced myself to write my character not the way I wished I had been, but how I really was – all the messy guilt and troubled truths to boot – resting in the knowledge that I too could write myself out of the darkness if I could learn to dwell and find the poetry in it first. Through this writing I have become more comfortable both in who I was and who I am. I've been able to talk to my mother with more clarity and support about her cancer. I've learned to be both more careful and more open in my friendships and to be more assertive as a reporter.

A few weeks from the time I'm writing this, I received a call from an unknown Boston number. I was at a dollar store in the Bronx, working on a deep-dive feature for *The New York Times*'s Metro section. Radio music was playing so loudly I couldn't hear the man on the other end of the line. I ducked outside. Over the wail of a nearby train, I heard the man identifying himself as the editor-in-chief of *The Boston Globe*. He was calling to congratulate me and a colleague for receiving a fellowship to finish a project we had worked on for over a year, then without the promise of publication: a data-heavy series on the country's broken child welfare system. The $100,000 grant, endowed by Hollywood, funds a year of investigative reporting with *The Boston Globe*'s Spotlight team.

Before starting my novel, I was not in a place to share these stories of abuse and neglect. I had done the research, collected the data, combed through thousands of documents noting deaths by abuse across the country; I was prepared from a reporting standpoint but not from a personal one. I was too removed even from myself to see anything else with the clarity and exactitude necessary for investigative journalism. But through writing, I came to a place of self-understanding and acceptance, ready to delve back into the darkness and to find meaning – this time in the lives and deaths of others.

***

Reading these responses from Alaina and Emily gave me new life. I'd been so stuck in a job that was sapping the joy out of me, drip by drip. I'd fallen victim to the same kind of mentality that was paralyzing so many of my students: the present ruled over everything. I couldn't think about the future. I couldn't see how lucky I was to have a life that was rich beyond my wildest dreams. But with every email from my former students, I realized that my life did not exist within the narrow walls of Room 413, Jordan High School, Durham, NC. It existed far beyond these walls.

Last year Emily came by my class for a visit. The 2016 election had just ended, and Emily was still pretty drained from working overtime at the *New York Times*. But she was happy to talk to my students about writing.

It is one thing for a teacher to say that writing is hard. It is a lot more helpful for students to hear it from someone who is there on the front lines, struggling to get by – even at the most respected newspaper in the country.

Emily pointed to her old seat and chuckled at the same scratch marks and stains that were there when she was a student. She was all grown up now, but my room remained the same. Now a new student sat in Emily's old desk. My job was to help this student grow up as well. The cycle was already set in motion.

I recently started to add up the numbers. Since 2005, over 1,800 students have taken my creative writing classes. That's 57 total classes, and I've compiled a published anthology for each class. 12,000 pages of stories, memoirs, and poetry. Over 2.5 million words in print.

But numbers aren't people. They don't tell stories, and if you don't attach a human face to these numbers, they quickly lose their meaning.

The four students I've introduced in this section – first George and Siddiq, and then Alaina and Emily – are as different as night and day. They come from broken homes and stable families, from vastly different circumstances, belief systems, intellectual gifts and interests. Their stories remind me to be present with my current students in their daily struggles and successes. Their stories also remind me to see their endless future possibilities.

When we serve others, we have to walk this fine line. We have to live in the here and now. We also have to see beyond the horizon. These two ideas go hand in hand, the present dictating the future and the future unfolding before us if our eyes are open to the possibilities.

Every year in my creative writing classes, I do a lesson on creativity and reinvention. I introduce a poetry technique called Newspaper Blackout, where my students take a page of text – a newspaper article, an advertisement, any text will do – and they cross out everything but a select number of words scattered across the page, creating a new poem that is nothing like the original text. I challenge them to look at a page of text and forget about the intended order of the words. Then I ask them to imagine certain words lifting off of the page, glowing brightly until they reconnect with the other floating words to create something brand new, something exciting and original.

Musicians do this all the time when they sample an older song. They take a familiar tune or a choral structure and they reuse it in a whole new way. An old jazz melody gets reconstructed into hip-hop. Bluegrass gives way to heavy metal. The old becomes new again.

Anne Lamott once wrote that "Life is like a recycling center, where all the concerns and dramas of humankind get recycled back and forth across the universe. But what you have to offer is your own sensibility."

Lamott's words really resonate with me. And when I think about reinvention, my mind goes beyond the creation of poems or songs. I try to see my students like a jumbled page of text. They are a vessel, a body that is set upon a specific path, but their final form is largely unknown. When I look at them I think about all of the paths they can take, who they will become, how they will respond to the inevitable joys and sorrows of life. I try to lift their good qualities above the page, backlit so that I can really see them, so that I can remember the good when the bad tries to take over. I shuffle them around, reimagining who they will become in the future. I create a new story out of these glowing pieces.

We should do this with every person we truly care about. It is not enough to simply see the good in someone. We need to take the next step of lifting that person up so that their goodness can shine brightly. We know that the bad is just lingering in the shadows, waiting to infect us if we're not careful, if someone doesn't shine a bright enough light.

People aren't poems, and they're not songs. I know this. But I think there's a lesson here.

We are flawed creatures. We do stupid things all the time, allowing other people to tell us who we are and who we are meant to be. But it doesn't have to be that way. We don't have to tear other people down; we can build them up and let them shine to their full potential. Then we can step back and know that we have done something good. Something right.

And no one has to give us credit for it. Validation doesn't matter anymore. We do this selfless act because nothing in the world matters more than lifting up another human being. It's not about ego. It's not about pride. It's simply about being good.

#9

Leadership

I never thought of myself as much of a leader.

Growing up, I was an introvert. I thought leaders were the kind of people who stood in front of a crowd and looked confident. They persuaded others by the sheer force of their personality. They were louder than the rest, spontaneous, always able to put on their game face even when things weren't going well. Leaders were visibly strong. They exuded power.

Now I'm not so sure. Yes, there are plenty of effective leaders who are extroverts. And yes, we live in a society where those who project power often use their power, whether it is real or imagined, to influence those who are weak. But leadership is more complicated than that.

I used to be in awe of people who could speak comfortably in front of a large group. Apparently I'm not alone; studies show us that humans are typically more afraid of public speaking than they are of death. As a kid I didn't understand how much vulnerability it took to stand in front of a large group of people while they watched your every move.

I never wanted to be on a stage like that. I did have my own opinions, though. I also couldn't stand it when a group of people refused to help someone who was being marginalized. This rubbed me the wrong way because I felt like an outsider most of the time. Maybe we all do at some point in our lives. If someone could have reassured me that I wasn't alone, that we all feel disconnected from time to time, I probably would have been a much happier kid.

When I was in middle school, I went to a predominately white private school. At the beginning of sixth grade, an Indian kid named Arvin joined our class. He was awkward and chubby. He wore thick-rimmed glasses. He sweated a lot and had poor personal hygiene. Nobody in my class wanted to have anything to do with him.

I was embarrassed for Arvin. I'd been raised well enough to recognize that he had to be incredibly lonely. New school. New surroundings. No friends to speak of and no chance at making any new friends for the foreseeable future.

So I tried to make him feel welcome. But as soon as I befriended Arvin, he latched on to me with every fiber of his being. He followed me everywhere. I knew I was doing the right thing, but it felt lonely doing the right thing because nobody wanted to hang out with me anymore. Sure, I was helping Arvin, but what about *my* social life? Why was I being punished for being kind to the new kid?

Eventually I gave in to my peers. I was never mean to Arvin, but if I saw him coming my way, I walked in the opposite direction. I was polite to him but rarely engaged with him in any kind of meaningful way. I never found out much about where he was from, or what brought his family to our small southern town, or what it was like to have brown skin in a school full of white people.

I was a coward back then.

For a moment, though, I caught a glimpse of what it can look like to serve someone else. I could have been a leader. I could have stuck with Arvin and learned more about him. Maybe I could have helped him to fit in a little better and to pick up on a few social cues. If I had stayed present with Arvin, even when I didn't want to, eventually my friends would have accepted him. But I didn't have the courage to wait out the discomfort.

To serve others, sometimes we have to risk being lonely. We have to put ourselves out there without knowing what will happen. We have to be confident in our knowledge of right and wrong. We need to be brave. We need to stand up for those who are weak. We have to embody what we want others to become. People are inspired by vulnerability. It takes courage to admit that we're not perfect. And while kindness and compassion are inherently good, they are not easy to live out on a daily basis. Sometimes we need a little nudge. I could have nudged my friends to accept Arvin into our class, but I didn't. I regret it to this day.

Leadership can take many forms. Sometimes the quietest people can wield the most influence. They lead by example. They inspire others by their presence. Sometimes we need the loudest voice in the room to bring us to our senses. But whether you are an extrovert or an introvert, service requires us to step out of our skins and to meet the needs of people where they are. What do they want? How can we serve them more effectively? Then we have to listen carefully to what they have to say. Only then can we decide whether to take up the bullhorn or to slip into the shadows.

The best classes I have taught typically have one thing in common: someone steps forward in a courageous way to honor a classmate who is not like them. They take a risk. Sure, I can create a safe environment for someone to step forward, but I can't take the step for them. Most people are followers. I know that's a negative view of humanity, but think about it: when you see someone step forward in a courageous way, how does it make you feel? Inspired, probably, because servant leadership is a rare and precious thing. I wish this wasn't the case. I wish more people would step forward instead of lingering in the shadows. I have to believe that we can do better.

These days I've accepted my role as a leader. I lead my two sons through their childhoods. I lead my students and football players and fellow teachers by my example. I don't have a booming voice and I can't command a room with my presence, but I'm willing to step out front without knowing how things will turn out. I want people to see me and know that I will put their interests ahead of my own. That I will take a risk. And if I fall flat on my face while everyone is watching, I will pick myself back up and do it again, because taking a risk is the right thing to do.

#10
Humility

It's not about me. It's not about me. It's not about me...

If I say this enough times, perhaps I will start to believe it. Then where will I be? I don't know. I will live in the same skin, breath the same air, go about my life in much the same way. But I will be different. The arc of my life will slowly bend toward new possibilities. I will do a better job of being present with my family. Perhaps I will see new opportunities to help people. Every day will be a blank canvas brimming with possibilities.

The psychologist Mihaly Csikszentmihalyi speaks to this idea in his book *Flow*:

"If one operates with unself-conscious assurance, and remains open to the environment and involved in it, a solution is likely to emerge. The process of discovering new goals in life is in many respects similar to that by which an artist goes about creating an original work of art. Whereas a conventional artist starts painting a canvas knowing what she wants to paint, and holds to her original intention until the work is finished, an original artist with equal technical training commences with a deeply felt but undefined goal in mind, keeps modifying the picture in response to the unexpected colors and shapes emerging on the canvas, and ends up with a finished work that probably will not resemble anything she started out with."

This is true for creativity and it is true for life. We have to let go of control if we are ever going to embrace the possibilities that come our way.

Csikszentmihalyi continues: "If the artist is responsive to her inner feelings, knows what she likes and does not like, and pays attention to what is happening on the canvas, a good painting is bound to emerge. On the other hand, if she holds on to a preconceived notion of what the painting should look like, without responding to the possibilities suggested by the forms developing before her, the painting is likely to be trite."

As a high school athlete, I was already familiar with the concept of "flow." In sports, it is the moment when you feel completely immersed in a game. The world fades away and the task at hand is right in front of you, shining under a spotlight. You are calm and focused and completely alive in the moment. Csikszentmihalyi and other scholars argue that this feeling can apply to almost everything we do. Flow is about living in the here and now, being purposeful, being present to such a degree that time passes by almost effortlessly. It is an incredible feeling.

So why do we not live like this more often? We all want to have a purpose in life, but when the time comes to make this happen, we usually give in to our worst impulses. We get selfish. We seek affirmation from other people instead of serving other people. There's a big difference between these two concepts. If we spend our lives feeding off of praise instead of lifting people up, we will always end up feeling hollow inside. Praise is never enough. Status is never enough. The most consistent path to lasting joy involves humility.

It's not about me. It's not about me. It's not about me...

Earlier in the book, I mentioned that I rarely get sick during the school year. In 17 years, I have only missed a handful of work days because of illness.

But over the summer, my body completely falls apart. I get rashes on my face, kidney stones, digestive issues, you name it – all the weird stuff that is embarrassing and uncomfortable and lingers for days on end. I obsess over these ailments because I finally have the free time to obsess over them. So instead of enjoying my summer break from school, I wallow in self-pity and feel annoyed a good bit of the time.

Summers and holidays also tend to be the time when my dad gets sick. This past winter he spent two months in the hospital starting on Christmas Eve. Then two more months over the summer. With my boys in tow, I made the two and a half hour trip down I-85 from Durham to Gastonia to see him. I spent day after day in his hospital room helping him to eat or change his position in bed, feeling the stress in the back of my temple every time my dad took a ragged breath. Time passed by in a haze. I couldn't shake the smell of disinfectant, the sound of the TV blaring constantly, the beeping monitors. The world outside my dad's 5th floor window unfolded with green trees and passing cars while I stayed in one place, not sure if my dad would ever get out of this hospital room alive.

These kinds of moments are humbling. We feel like we're in control until our body rebels against us for no good reason, or a loved one gets sick and there's nothing we can do to make their pain go away. Obstacles like this will hit some of us harder than others. As annoying as my summer ailments are, they could be much worse. I need to accept them and move on. I can't make my dad's illnesses go away, so I should just treasure every moment I get to spend with him. We're all on borrowed time, and none of us are guaranteed tomorrow.

I want to get better at this. I want to come home from a long day of work and be completely present with my family. I want to be able to laugh when I get sick instead of wallowing in self-pity. Life is beautiful and life is short. Why do I have to keep reminding myself of this?

Maybe that's the point. The act of remembering is an act of humility. We are not always in control. Tragedy can strike us at any moment. This is scary, and many of us choose to live in fear or to avoid living at all. If I don't take any risks, I won't have to feel the sting of disappointment. If I love someone deeply, won't that inevitably lead to loss? People will always let you down in the end.

I refuse to live like this. I want to cherish everything. I want to keep my feet firmly planted to the ground. I want to put the spotlight on someone else and bring a smile to their face. I will no longer crave any attention because I will be fully alive in the moment. It will be someone else's moment, but it will also be my moment.

Kate Bowler is a respected professor at Duke. After years of trying to have a baby, she was finally blessed with a healthy boy. She had the kind of charmed life that so many of us aspire to. Then she received a stage-4 cancer diagnosis. In her memoir *Everything Happens for a Reason*, Bowler wrestles with how to live after her world gets turned upside down.

"I would not say it was simply that I didn't stop to smell the roses," she writes. "It was the sin of arrogance, of being impervious to life itself. I failed to love what was present and decided to love what was possible instead. I must learn to live in ordinary time, but I don't know how."

She doesn't know how. I don't know how. None of us knows how to be fully present. For me, the sin of arrogance comes when I think I have everything figured out. That's usually when life knocks me to the ground.

No one understands this feeling better than addicts. So many people struggle with an addiction, whether it's to drugs or alcohol or gambling or sex. But addiction can take many more forms. We can also be addicted to ambition, money, attention, or power. Addiction creeps up on us like a vine until it strangles the life out of us.

In 1939 the Twelve Step Program was developed for Alcoholics Anonymous. These twelve steps have stood the test of time, and the founding principles have been used to conquer many other forms of addiction. The process overlaps with our discussion of service. First, an addict must give up control and admit that he can no longer handle his problem. Then he has to recognize his past errors and make amends for these errors. Once he has done this, he can begin to live by a new code, shaping his life in a radical new way – almost as if he has been reborn as a different human being. Then comes the final and most important step: the addict must agree to help others down the path to recovery. He has to serve others.

He has to live outside of himself in a way that binds himself to the world at large. That's when he will feel a sense of purpose. That's when his recovery will become transformational. Life will feel richer, fuller, more beautiful. He will have the emotional armor to fight off worry and the Seduction of the Self.

Addiction is the kind of mental prison that plagues so many of us. When our mind is shackled, our humanity is lost. We are surrounded by concrete walls that block our view of what is possible. Life has no color, no immediacy. Why get up in the morning if there is nothing to engage in or to think about? We need to experience the wonder and beauty that will inevitably come when we serve people.

But we can't do this without first admitting that we have a problem. The problem is us, our ego, our addiction to the Self. We need to serve people, and we need to be grateful for those people who serve us.

All of this involves humility. When we free ourselves to admit that we don't have everything under control, we can begin our lives anew. Anything is possible.

It's not about me. It's not about me. It's not about me…

It's about so much more than me.

Why is this shift so important?

There are things that we want, and there are things that we need.

My son Brett learned about this concept in his second grade classroom. If an eight-year-old can grasp it, so can the rest of us. I want a new car, but I don't need a new car. I want to sleep late and skip work, but I need the income to pay my bills. These differences are clear, but the gap between wants and needs isn't always straightforward. I want to be respected in my profession, but do I need to be praised in order to do my job well? I want to make a lasting impact on the world, but do I need to pursue this kind of lofty ambition in order to feel like a successful adult? Life is full of these choices. They influence our careers, our habits, and our most basic reasons for waking up in the morning.

In 1943 the psychologist Abraham Maslow created an influential framework for the full range of human motivations. According to Maslow's Hierarchy of Needs, once our basic needs are met (breathing, food, shelter, etc.), an emotionally healthy person can move on to the kinds of needs that make for a rich and productive life. These needs include safety, love, esteem, and self-actualization. In a nutshell, self-actualization means that we try to become the best possible version of ourselves, striving to understand ourselves and to serve others. True happiness resides at the top of this pyramid.

As I have previously mentioned, moving from an inward mindset to an outward mindset is incredibly difficult. The Seduction of the Self is powerful. Addictions are powerful. There are plenty of reasons why it is hard to be empathetic or humble or comfortable in our own skin. But the advantages of a life of service far outweigh the drawbacks. Here are just a few of these advantages:

1. When you serve someone, any attention you get is indirect – thus, your intent is much more likely to be pure.
2. Service makes other people happy.
3. Service gives you a level of satisfaction that you could never achieve on your own.
4. Service gives your life a purpose because there is always more work to be done.

1. When you serve someone, any attention you get is indirect – thus, your intent is much more likely to be pure.

Something happens to us when we receive a physical reward for doing the right thing. We come to expect this kind of reward, and doing the right thing becomes a transactional experience. This is helpful when we are children. Our brains are still developing, and sometimes we need physical triggers to understand a concept. If you touch a hot stove, you feel pain; if you do something nice for your classmate at school, you get a certificate or a piece of candy. This feels good, so we associate altruism with a quick dopamine rush. As we get older, we are able to (hopefully) see the benefits of serving others outside of a physical reward.

But let's be real here. It's not easy to be selfless. We have to fight against an entire culture that encourages self-promotion and self-centeredness. We want the spotlight on us because it feels good, or at least we think it feels good, in the way that a sugar rush feels good or a bunch of social media "likes" feels good. But the spotlight gives us a fleeting happiness, and it certainly doesn't fill us with anything close to joy.

What if we put the spotlight on someone else, lifting up someone's spirits when they were down or shining a light on someone's talents? You will feel good about this moment because it wouldn't exist without your help. You won't need the spotlight shining down on you in order to sustain that feeling; the warm glow will remain long after the spotlight fades away, working on your heart like the best kind of addiction – the kind that comes when you put a smile on someone's face.

2. Service makes other people happy.

Happiness is a communal act. As I said earlier, try watching a funny movie by yourself and see if your laughter doesn't feel a bit hollow. We feed off of other people. I love to hear noise in my classroom because noise equals energy, and energy is the only thing that will keep a teenager awake in the morning. We respond to the things we hear and the things we see around us. No one likes to be around people who complain all the time. They sap the positive energy out of a room.

No matter how I am feeling at the beginning of a school day, I will stand at my door smiling as my students enter the room. Sometimes my smile comes easy. Other times, it is hard. I put on a fake smile even when I'm not happy – especially when I am not happy, because my students will feed off of my negativity. Usually they respond to my optimism by being optimistic in return, which means that even when I start the day with a fake smile, it eventually turns into something genuine.

It can be hard to make someone happy, but we have to live this way. Our work will feel less like work, our life will have a heightened sense of purpose, and our daily interactions will become all the more meaningful.

I love to watch my wife laugh. Her smile brightens her face and brings out the warmth in her eyes, making her all the more beautiful to me. When Brett and Cason smile, their faces are full of wonder because the world is so new and vibrant to them, unfolding like a new adventure every single day.

It is easy to watch our loved ones smile. It is even more transformative to watch someone smile when you know they have a really difficult life. Happiness is a rare privilege to them, and worry sticks around like an old friend. But when we serve that person, we have the power to take their worries away, at least for a short period of time. We have the power to lift them up, make them smile, ease their burdens, and help them to know that they are not alone. We don't need some kind of tangible reward when we do this. The smile is enough.

It is always enough, especially when we serve people on a regular basis. Their smiles become our smiles, warming our hearts and reminding us that living for others is undeniably beautiful.

3. Service gives you a level of satisfaction that you could never achieve on your own.

I like to accomplish things. I create lists at the beginning of the day, and it makes me happy to cross off these items at the end of the day. Crossing off a task means that my brain is free from one more burden. My life feels more efficient.

But my brain still remains cluttered. One task goes away and another one takes its place. My thoughts function like a constantly moving conveyor belt, always presenting the next task to be completed. I rarely feel settled or at peace.

At times like this, I try to go outside. I take in the fresh air, feel the wind at my face, watch the trees and the squirrels dancing along the highest limbs. I remind myself that the world exists outside of my own head. Nature helps me to fold outward, at least temporarily.

Service makes this process more permanent. People are not tasks. They are not items to be checked off of a list, only to be discarded once they are no longer useful. When you help someone without expecting anything in return, the world not only feels bigger but it also feels deeper, more complete. It's kind of like exercise, or any work that pushes your body to exhaustion. Your body aches in the moment, but afterwards you feel calm and relaxed. Your thoughts are focused and simplified, your muscles break down and grow a little bit stronger, your chest rises and falls with steady breaths. The good feeling lingers for days to come.

Service has the same effect. When we live for someone else, the feeling stays with us afterwards. We remember these moments because the memory is not about us. We can actually *see* the good that results from our work, rather than the temporary high of self-indulgence. Yes, we still have to take care of ourselves; I am simply asking us to reassess the way that we take care of ourselves. We have to look outward even when we are taking care of our own body. I'm motivated to eat well and to exercise so that I have more energy to play with my children. I love to learn new things because knowledge allows me to serve people in new and creative ways. I love to experience the arts because music and movies remind me that the world is full of immense beauty.

"To live as if we are dying gives us a chance to experience some real presence," Anne Lamott writes. "Time is so full for people who are dying in a conscious way, full in the way that life is for children. They spend big round hours."

When I read this passage to my students I like to ask them a revealing question: If you knew that you were going to die tomorrow, what would you do today?

Some of my students immediately turn inward: they'd go out in a blaze of glory, experimenting with drugs or sky diving or tempting death in some other way. But most of my students say that on their last day, they'd like to be present with the people they care about. They would serve someone else, knowing that this final act of kindness will give their lives permanence long after they are gone. Otherwise, why live in the first place? Who wants to enter this world as a burden and then leave without making some kind of positive impact? At moments like this, I feel good about the future of our country. Young people want to be good.

4. Service gives your life a purpose because there is always more work to be done.

We all need a reason to get up in the morning. When people retire after a lifetime of work, their future happiness and health will likely depend on their sense of purpose going forward.

Is there still work to be done? Does my life have a purpose outside of work? How can I be of service to others? Is anyone counting on me right now? If not, what can I do to change this dynamic?

So what does it mean to have a sense of purpose? It's not about financial security. After a certain point, money doesn't make us happy. In a 2018 study in the journal *Nature Human Behavior*, researchers pulled data from a Gallop World Poll survey of over 1.7 million participants from 164 countries to determine that people are happiest when they make about $75,000 a year. At $75,000 our basic needs can be met, and any income beyond that point will not have a lasting impact on our well-being. A 2007 study in the *Journal of Academic Psychology* asked why most people who achieve major life goals like winning the lottery don't wind up being happier in the long run. The answer: winning the lottery can make a major difference in your financial situation, but ultimately it will not affect your relationships or your basic approach to life. If you had a negative attitude before winning the lottery, the study says, you will continue to have a negative attitude after winning the lottery.

That's why it is so important to have something – or someone – to focus on. If we commit to helping others, we will constantly be reminded that there is more work to do. Poverty and brokenness are firmly entrenched in the fabric of our daily lives. This can be overwhelming if we think about it in the wrong way. After all, can our own efforts really make a difference in the world? The problems are too big. The needs are too great. Sure, we can live like this, and plenty of people do. We can avoid stepping into the mess, and yes, it's a mess that can sap our energy and make us feel helpless.

Or we can look at service differently. Children are taught to see mistakes with a growth mindset – mistakes are a necessary part of life, paving the way for new learning. Why can't we look at service in the same way? The world is broken. I am broken. We are all broken. That's not going to change. My time on this planet is finite; I can choose to be consumed by this brokenness or I can get out of bed in the morning and help someone anyway. This may not be an "efficient" use of our time. We may not see any tangible results for years to come. But we will know that when we get out of bed, our day has a purpose. It is full. And when we wake up the next morning, we will get out of bed with the same sense of purpose. That sense of purpose will grow every day, with every kind word that we say and with every person we lift up.

Part III:
Where do we go from here?

Who do we serve?

For whatever reason, my house has become the unofficial playground for our neighborhood.

I love the noise of a yard filled with kids, the older ones engaged in an elaborate Nerf war as they run through the woods behind our house, the little ones pulling toys out of our garage (or making toys out of our yard equipment.) The whole yard looks like a war zone at the end of the day, the driveway covered in chalk drawings and toys scattered everywhere.

In the coming years these little kids will grow into big kids, and many of them will take my class if I can stick around long enough to last that long. I've either taught or coached most of the older kids on our street. This can be a wonderful thing, although I always feel like I have to be on my best behavior – I'm never going to cut my grass shirtless in the heat of summer, for example, knowing that half of Jordan High School could be driving by my house.

Being a good neighbor is a simple thing. A whole bunch of families have gotten to observe me over the years, and they've never expected anything magical; they just want me to be consistent, fair, and caring to their kids. That's it. Like I said, basic stuff. But trust takes years to build up. I have to show up for these people again and again with a smile on my face, treating all of my students with dignity. These kinds of opportunities are all around me. They are all around us.

I've spent a lot of time talking about the obstacles to service, along with the necessary qualities for this kind of work. I've tried to point out all the ways that I've struggled to integrate service into my life. I am nothing special. My perspective isn't particularly unique. But I want to shine a light on the world around me, and service is the best way to go about this important work.

We don't have to be special in order to serve others. We just have to recognize the opportunities around us every day. We can serve our co-workers, our neighbors, our friends, and our family. If each of us makes an effort to serve the people around us in our own small ways, we will see very real changes in our communities.

Here's some good news: most of us are already doing this kind of work. But we don't realize how much more we could be doing.

This was a revelation to me. The more I thought about service, the more I realized that I *was* serving other people, sometimes in small ways, sometimes in big ways. This is an important step, because how can I see the innate goodness in other people without looking for it in myself? I can be really hard on myself, focusing on all the ways that I don't measure up, obsessing over my failures. All of us do this from time to time. But as I thought about my success stories, I began to see them not as case stories for bragging, but as a way to identify where I'm on the right track so that I can go deeper in that direction. We shouldn't take the good things we do for granted. Instead, we need to recognize these good things and amplify them, while looking for new opportunities to put our abilities to good use.

So where do we go from here? That's the focus of Part III.

I want to look at all the ways we can serve the people we see on a regular basis. I don't have some kind of innovative formula or groundbreaking new system. Instead, I'll focus on real people and the kind of real situations that impact all of us. We have to dig deeper, to amplify the things we do well and to recognize the opportunities that are right there in front of us.

As we move towards service, what will "success" look like? We have to be careful here, grounding our actions in humility and serving others the way *they* want to be served.

The theologian Henri Nouwen writes, "When we start being too impressed by the results of our work, we slowly come to the erroneous conviction that life is one large scoreboard where someone is listing the points to measure our worth…The more we allow our accomplishments — the results of our actions — to become the criteria of our self-esteem, the more we are going to walk on our mental and spiritual toes, never sure if we will be able to live up to the expectations which we created by our last successes."

For Nouwen, success meant leaving his comfortable job as a professor at Harvard and spending the remaining years of his life at L'Arche, a French community for people with profound developmental disabilities.

"When you are able to create a lonely place in the middle of your actions and concerns," Nouwen writes, "your successes and failures slowly can lose some of their power over you. For then your love for this world can merge with a compassionate understanding of its illusions. Then your serious engagement can merge with an unmasking smile. Then your concern for others can be motivated more by their needs than your own. In short: then you can care."

You cannot truly care for someone unless you put your own needs aside. You have to get your baggage out of the way, cast it aside, leave it in the attic as you go about serving people.

Opportunities for service are all around us. Let's look at a few ways to go about this important work.

Profession

This year, I am serving as a mentor to one of our new English teachers, Alec. He is smart, capable, and an incredibly hard worker. He's also one of my former students.

I keep a running list of former students who have gone into teaching. Some of them are working in elementary schools; others are college professors. One of the advantages of working at a school for a long time is that former students come back to visit me often. I hear about their recent marriages, kids, job changes – all the milestones that begin in young adulthood and continue, in one form or another, for the rest of their lives.

Currently, 19 of my former students have gone into teaching. I wish there were more, because we need good people in education. But this job is not for everybody. The pay isn't great. The first few years are incredibly stressful. When I met with Alec the other day, he was slumped over and he looked tired. He had a stack of 70 ungraded essays beside him. He was trying to keep this job from consuming him, but he was losing the battle.

"It gets better," I said to him.

Alec gave me a weary smile. "That's what people keep telling me."

Alec is wise beyond his years. As a sophomore in my creative writing class, he acted more mature than most of my seniors. As a student at Princeton, he quickly became a leader on the school's poetry slam team, winning national awards along the way. He could have done anything, gone anywhere, but he chose to come back to his hometown, inspiring a new generation of students at his old high school.

Alec is innovative and he is grounded. He's already a good teacher, and I hope he can stick around long enough to stop drowning. As a mentor teacher, I'm supposed to lift Alec up when he's down. That role extends to all of the new teachers at my school, as well as my students. I constantly have to remind my stressed out students that everything is going to be okay. "Just chill out," I tell them. "Life gets better."

They look at me like I'm crazy sometimes. *How is this going to get any better?* The world seems to be closing in on them and nothing will make it better.

I give them a reassuring smile. "Yes it will. It always gets better."

I think about myself at their age. Everything was bright and scary and real, always incredibly real. So many new things were hitting me in waves that never seemed to let up long enough to catch my breath. The future was scary. The present was even scarier.

I take the long view now, a perspective that only comes with age. I recently turned 40, which is the kind of milestone that no one wants to celebrate. Eighteen is a big deal. So is 21.

Thirty is still okay. But when you turn 40 you are officially old. It doesn't bother me too much; instead of feeling like my life is halfway over (if I'm lucky enough to live that long,) I like to think of it as an opportunity. I've made plenty of mistakes in my 40 years, and I've learned plenty of lessons from these mistakes. When I look at my older co-workers, I see them as a treasure-trove of knowledge to pull from. How do you survive 30-40 years in this profession? How do you survive that long in *any* profession, for that matter? They look at me with the same knowing smile I give to my stressed-out students.

The people we work with can make our jobs so much easier if we take the time to learn from them. Usually their wisdom is hard earned and much more practical than anything we can learn in a textbook. Plus, people like to help their co-workers. It gives them a sense of dignity. They know that they matter as they tell me a story from their past. They feel known, and as I receive their wisdom, I also feel known.

Now I'm one of the veteran teachers, with gray hairs sprouting from my eyebrows, walking on aching knees and fighting tooth and nail to stay energized in spite of my body's inevitable decline. Working with teenagers keeps me young at heart. Serving them keeps me grounded; it's hard to complain about getting old when the people you serve make you feel alive. Sure, teenagers get swept up in way too much drama, but listen to the way they talk about music, or watch their faces light up as they talk about a new crush. They are alive in the way that adults used to be alive but can only vaguely remember.

This year, 65 kids signed up to take my advanced writing class. Over the course of a year, each of them will try to write an entire novel. They will live with the same set of characters and circumstances for nine straight months, sitting down to write every single day, even when they don't feel inspired and the task at hand seems almost impossible. Kids usually don't attempt this sort of thing. Neither do adults. It's easy to say, "I've got a great idea for a book. It can't be too hard." Talk is cheap, though. Claiming you have the skill to take on a challenge is one thing, but doing it is a whole different ballgame.

I've taught this novel-writing class for the past couple of years, and it's one of the most rewarding parts of my job. I get to guide a kid through this incredible challenge, cheering them on when their spirits are low and pushing them to work harder when they get complacent. Some of my budding novelists know exactly where they want to take their story. Many of them do not. I love to roll up my sleeves and help them think through their ideas. And they've got tons of ideas swirling around in their head. This is something that most adults don't understand about teenagers; we often think that young people are empty vessels waiting to be filled with knowledge from on high, but that's not really true. The ideas are already there, floating around in a disjointed way, and some of these ideas are more sophisticated than others. But they already exist in a teenager's brain. Sometimes they just need a teacher to help them access these ideas. That's where I come in.

By the end of the year, most of my novelists will have written at least 32,000 words. For some, that's the final goal. Their book will sit on a computer file or in a desk drawer as a testament to their high school years. No one else will read it, but that's not the point; the point is that they tried something hard and stuck with it for months on end, even when they wanted to give up. And when they read a good book in the future, they will understand just how hard it is to write a good book.

Every year, a handful of my students want to go a step further. They surpass their word count and keep on writing. At this point the grade doesn't matter anymore. They want to finish their book because it means something to them. I wish school could be like this for every kid – learning purely for the sake of learning, creating something tangible that truly represents who you are at a particular moment in time. I begin to feel less like their teacher and more like their colleague. They like this dynamic because it reminds them that they are growing up, taking on real responsibilities and discovering a distinct voice that will carry them into adulthood.

This is the point when the process really gets fun for me. I take their finished document – a year's worth of headaches and hard work – and I place it into a professional-looking template. Together we come up with a good cover design, create an account so that any money they make goes directly to them, and then publish the book online.

I love to watch the thrill in their eyes when they hold the finished book in their hands. They swell with pride. Their mom usually cries. Their friends can't believe that they actually wrote a book. The spotlight is entirely on them, and I get to watch it all unfold. I'll come back to this idea again later because it's such a fitting metaphor for service – the director behind the curtain of a play, the mechanic who makes a car hum to life, the coach calling plays from the sidelines. Everyone sees the final product under the lights, while the real work gets done behind the scenes.

Service is an inherent part of my work as a teacher. I am paid to help young people. Most jobs aren't like this. I'm simply using my own experiences because that's what I know. I'm not saying that everyone needs to become a teacher. What I am saying is this: you will spend most of your waking hours at a job. If you are a lucky, it is a job that pays the bills. If you are really lucky, it is a job that you enjoy. But that's not the reality for most of us. I have a good job, but I don't enjoy my job all the time. If we spend our lives looking for work that fulfills us, we are bound to be disappointed. But our work can still be deeply satisfying.

From an early age we are encouraged to find something to be passionate about and to let this passion guide us down our career path. In his book *So Good They Can't Ignore You*, computer scientist Cal Newport makes a convincing counterargument: "If you want to love what you do," he writes, "abandon the passion mindset ('what can the world offer me?') and instead adopt the craftsman mindset ('what can I offer the world?') … Passion comes after you put in the hard work to become excellent at something valuable, not before. In other words, what you do for a living is much less important than how you do it."

For some people, the craftsman mindset involves honing your skills at a particular task, like welding or composing legal arguments. But a worker's "craft" can also be serving the people he or she works with on a regular basis. This does not have to be an entirely selfless endeavor. As workers, we need to fill our own tanks with creative endeavors not only to break up the monotony of work, but also to give us the necessary energy to be outward-facing. I love designing book covers in part because it taps into the creative impulses that don't get fed when I'm teaching. For the same reason I've been working to make a documentary film about my novel-writing students. It's a new challenge and yet another way to tap into my creativity. This gets me fired up, which carries over into every aspect of my teaching. I get to learn something new, and I get to use this knowledge to shine an even brighter light on my students. I've also learned a new skill that I can pass on to my co-workers.

When I was a football coach, my favorite players were the "glue guys." These weren't the best athletes; instead, they were the above average athletes who worked hard, had a positive attitude, and, most importantly, connected everyone together because of their humility. Players were drawn to these glue guys because they knew, deep down, that the team could not exist without them. They lifted everyone up. Most importantly, they served their teammates without asking for anything in return. This is a powerful example for teenagers to follow, and it is a powerful example for us to follow in the working world.

As a kid, being on a team gave me a sense of purpose. It gave me friends, kept me from being lonely, and kept me from focusing on myself all the time. Why can't we take this same mindset to our professional lives? We should lift up the people we work with. Make them smile. Make them feel valued. We don't have to love everything about our co-workers – that's not the point. The point is that work is so much more enjoyable when we have a shared identity and a collective sense of purpose.

When I stopped coaching, I knew that I was really going to miss the relationships with my fellow coaches. LaDwaun Harrison and I spent 14 years on the practice field together. You really get to know someone when you show up for a common cause day after day, sweating in the heat of the sunshine and painting the game field well into the night. When we both resigned from coaching, I worried that our bond would weaken.

I should have had more faith in friendship. These days, instead of meeting on a football field, LaDwaun and I meet a couple times each week in my classroom. We still talk about football, but we also talk about our families, our hopes, and our fears. LaDwaun has helped me adjust to life without coaching, and I think that I have helped him as well. We've decided to stay at our school as teachers in spite of its imperfections. And by doing so, we have been able to overcome some of the hurt that occurred in those final months of coaching.

I've tried to be more open as a friend to the rest of my co-workers, from the new teachers like Alec to the veteran history teacher down the hall named Brian who, in addition to being one of the best teachers I know, has written a book about the desegregation of our school in the 1960s. I helped him get it published, and this book has made a positive impact on our school community. How many teachers are doing incredible things in the math wing or other parts of our school that I've never found the time to explore? I should reach out to them. In fact, I *will* reach out to them because while we may teach in the isolation of our own classrooms, we are only as strong as the bonds we create with each other.

Not all of us will be passionate about our jobs. But when we serve our co-workers, our jobs have a greater purpose. We'll still have to grind away at hard or tedious tasks. That's just life. But service gives our work meaning. It makes the grind bearable. It brings a smile to someone's face, and that, more than a big paycheck, will give us a reason to get out of bed in the morning.

Community

I love the ending of the second Harry Potter book, *The Chamber of Secrets*. Harry wonders why he wasn't placed in the Slytherin House when he first arrived at Hogwarts. The sorting hat wanted to place him there; after all, Harry was smart, cunning and ambitious – the kinds of traits that defined the Slytherins, who often found a way to bend these qualities in the service of evil. But this didn't feel right to Harry. Instead, he asked the sorting hat to place him in the Gryffindor House.

As the story unfolds, Harry feels like he is caught between two versions of himself. So he turns to the great wizard Dumbledore and asks for his advice.

Dumbledore smiles knowingly at Harry and says, "It is our choices, Harry, that show what we truly are, far more than our abilities."

Sometimes our choices are profound. They send us down very specific paths when it comes to work, marriage, where we live, and how we find meaning in the world. We make bad choices out of fear, or greed, or the nagging feeling that we don't measure up. We feel paralyzed by these decisions because the answer isn't always clear. Every path is filled with pitfalls or golden opportunities. There's no guidebook for any of this.

Sometimes our choices don't feel nearly as profound. We decide not to sell our house, or we smile at our neighbor every time we see them, or we offer a steady shoulder for someone to lean on when they need a helping hand. After a while, people start to trust us. They start to rely on us.

But being a good neighbor usually involves some extra work. After all, it's easier to shut the blinds and never open your front door. And let's be honest here: we're all busy; sometimes it's simply not convenient to stop and spend time with a neighbor, especially the old lady down the street who will talk for hours about her arthritis or her grandson in New Jersey. We don't really get anything tangible from these interactions – as if people were like vending machines and every good deed we did inevitably leads to a bag of salty chips. But this is a necessary part of life. We rush too much anyway; sometimes standing in place is just what we need to slow down, get over ourselves, and act like a decent human being.

As I've said before, though, we live in a complicated world. Not all people are good, and brokenness has a way of banging on our door whether we like it or not.

Every year or two, a series of break-ins will happen in my neighborhood. The response from my neighbors is fairly predictable: there's a lot of hand-wringing about safety, about being on the lookout for strangers walking down the street, about spending a bunch of money on home security systems. Our neighborhood is on edge.

We've got to be more careful. This could happen to anyone, any time.

I'm certainly guilty of this. One day when my son Brett was a baby, I came home from work and realized our house had been broken into. I gently placed Brett's carrier seat on the floor and walked through the house. It was a wreck. Every drawer had been opened up, the contents scattered everywhere. Even Brett's nursery was trashed. What were they going to find in a baby's drawers? Money? Jewelry?

I was furious. It felt like the sanctity of my family had been violated in some fundamental way. What if Jenni and Brett had been home when this happened? Something terrible could have happened to them. How can you trust people after something like this?

But we have to keep living. We have to put our anger away and decide to either live in fear or to welcome vulnerability, accepting all of the good and the bad that come from this option.

Our lives are full of choices, and fear can force us to avoid the kinds of interactions that make a community thrive. We need to step outside of our comfort zone. We need to take a risk, connecting with our neighbors and with the people who make up our city, especially those who are marginalized. It's not enough to give money to those who are struggling with poverty. Instead, we need to get to know these people, spending time with them, giving them a small slice of the dignity that was stripped from them so long ago. If you are a member of a faith community, don't just go to worship on Sundays.

Get to know your fellow congregants on a deeper level. Think of your hometown in much the same way. It is not enough to simply exist in a place; we need to be present in the world around us. Coach a youth sports team, join a civic group, rake an elderly person's yard. These are simple things that anyone can do. So often we avoid doing them because they *are* so simple.

What difference does it make? What difference does anything make?

It makes a profound difference.

Service can be simple. We may not want simple, because simple sounds boring, but a simple act done repeatedly, day after day, builds upon itself like a work of art – molding brown, boring clay into something beautiful, something that stands the test of time.

Earlier in this book I mentioned that people are becoming more and more skeptical of institutions. Some of this skepticism is well-earned. Our political climate is a mess. The Catholic church is reeling from decades of child-abuse among its clergy. Public schools are becoming more and more segregated. The gap between the rich and the poor is only growing wider, calling into question the very notion of the American Dream. Yes, some of our biggest institutions seem to be broken.

So let's fix them. Let's lean into this brokenness instead of running in the opposite direction.

I teach at a public school because, in spite of its imperfections, there is something profoundly good about working for an institution that is responsible for serving *everyone* who lives in a particular community, no matter what your race, socio-economic status, or intelligence may be.

I joined a church because of a deep, abiding faith in the power of praying side by side with fellow believers. Our church is so much more than a Sunday worship service. This commitment to community has been embodied over the past year in our church's relationship with Temple Beth El, a Jewish synagogue down the street. As Beth El has undergone renovations, they've used our church for all of their classes, services, and operations. On that first day of our partnership, they paraded down the street from Temple Beth El to our church in a moving ceremony, carrying the Torah at the front of the line and serving as a witness to all of downtown Durham that while we may worship God in different ways, our love for our neighbors will always stand on firm ground.

Our church has recently partnered with a local nonprofit called Durham CAN (Congregations Associations and Neighborhoods) which has done some impressive advocacy work around issues such as affordable housing, discrimination, and jobs. CAN organizes around a different issue each year, and they decide on this issue by holding a series of listening sessions across the city. For our church, this has involved countless one-on-one meetings between our congregants, with the goal of not only getting to know each other better, but also to understand the common hopes and dreams for our city. Basically, it's all about relationship-building.

This kind of work takes time. We've opened our doors to another faith community and we've opened our hearts to the people sitting in the pews beside us each Sunday, building trust and feeling more firmly rooted to an institution that is imperfect but still quite beautiful. We serve our community by opening our hearts to others. We listen. We don't pass judgment. We come to understand that our views may be different from some of the people in our community, but this is okay. A community will only flourish if its citizens feel that they have a place at the table.

Now, when I walk into our stately old sanctuary, I feel my faith take root in soil that is rich and deep. Durham has become more of a home to me. It is my community; it is a place where I belong. So many people don't have this sense of belonging. They long to feel known, and their anger and resentment grows with every year that they don't feel known. Religious institutions like a church or a mosque or a synagogue often provide that bridge between loneliness and trust, between isolation and belonging. These institutions are imperfect, but they merely represent the imperfections of all human beings. If we truly believe in the basic goodness in most people, we should be willing to give these organizations a chance. After all, our communities are only as strong as the institutions that bind us together.

These days I'm trying to embrace the everyday details of my daily life – the musty smell of my cinderblock classroom, the predictable drive home from work as I pass the same neighborhoods, the scuffed hardwood floors in my house and the tiny handprints on almost all of my windows. None of these things are particularly beautiful. We all experience these reminders of daily life, but we often don't appreciate them until they are taken away. In the moment they are simply a backdrop to more pressing matters.

I want to live my life differently. I want to celebrate the mundane details of each day. I want to breathe in the musty scent of my classroom and tell myself that this is the smell of a life-time of memories. The homes passing by my car window belong to families who are bound to this city in the same way that I am. The imperfections of my house are evidence of my sons' boundless energy. Everything comes alive to them. Why can't everything come alive to me as well?

I need to keep planting seeds. That's the thing about rooting yourself in a community; you have to stick around long enough to watch things grow. This takes time and attention. It takes sunshine and new seasons and renewal.

I need to stay put in the broken places and wait for the healing to begin.

It's been three years since I stopped coaching football. I'm still unhappy about the way things ended, but the bitterness has faded away. Now I can look back on those 14 years with pride. We helped a lot of boys grow into men. These days I run into my former players all around town: a pharmacist at CVS, a young parent during open house at my sons' elementary school, a police officer keeping the streets safe late at night. My former players are all around me.

Was I a good coach? I don't know. I'm not sure if that really matters anymore. But I know one thing for sure: I was present. My players knew that they could count on me to be there for them, day after day. I offered words of encouragement. I tried not to get frustrated when they did the stupid things that most teenagers do. I tried to treat them with dignity and maybe teach them a few lessons along the way. I wanted them to know that when they grew up and looked back on their adolescence, they could point to at least one adult who cared about them.

Many of my former players are surprised to learn that I'm still teaching after all these years. They still call me "Coach," and I let them call me coach because a part of me will always be a coach. But I have to keep telling myself that I am more than just a coach. I am many things, yet at the same time I am a very average human. I am one person in a city of 267,000, a state of 10.38 million, a country of 327 million. I am a neighbor, a Presbyterian, a Jordan Falcon, a Durhamite. I am all of these things, and I am connected by the many threads of this city. I really want to stay connected, and I want to help others be connected as well.

Maybe I'll go back into coaching someday. Maybe not. If I do, coaching will no longer define me. It will be just be one more way to serve the people around me.

Until then, I'll find other ways to dig my hands into the soil. I will try to be a good neighbor. I will try to help my community thrive. I will keep planting seeds until they grow into towering trees.

Friend

Becky was a good friend. She lived a few streets down from me in an old white house. She loved to watch the birds from her front porch, so I came over once a week to water her plants, fill up the bird feeder, and sit with her in the shade. I usually brought my boys along, and Becky loved to give them vanilla ice cream for a treat.

Becky and I had a lot in common. She was a huge North Carolina Tar Heel fan – she even painted her car Carolina blue. She loved to laugh too; her mouth would open wide and her head would tilt back while she clapped her hands together. She was old and frail, but her mind was incredibly sharp. She was kind, too; Becky and I weren't related, but she treated me, my wife, and our two boys like family.

Becky lived a full life. I didn't get to know her until the last ten years. At that point she needed help with the birds, her plants, and the trash each week. She lived alone until the very end.

Spending time with Becky wasn't always convenient. I was usually tired at the end of the work day, and the only thing

I wanted to do was go home, change into some comfortable clothes, and have dinner with my family. But Becky needed help. Plus, isn't that what friends do for each other?

Becky was always happy to see us. I'd sit with her on the porch while the boys played in the yard. Cason would find a good stick and use it to fight imaginary monsters. Brett liked to pace back and forth, letting his mind unwind from another busy day at school. Becky watched them with a smile on her face. She liked to tell me about the young mother who jogged past her house every morning, pushing a stroller. Around 8:05 a.m. the school bus would arrive to pick up her neighbor's kids. After that, Becky would do some more bird watching, then a few shows on TV, then an afternoon nap. Her days were limited but satisfying.

Sometimes I envied Becky. My days were anything but simple; my head was usually swimming with things to do, places to be. But every week Becky forced me to put these plans on hold and just sit there, taking in the world around me. I learned to be present in the moment, listening to Becky as she told me about her day. I was able to help her feel more alive with each story. I guess that's what friendship is all about: honoring someone's humanity. This can be an incredible gift, but we don't realize it is a gift until someone takes it away.

All across our communities, people like Becky are alone. We may not know they are alone because we see them every day. We may even nod to them, or make small talk with them about the weather. But we don't really *see* them. It takes time to really see someone. We have to be present with them through their joy and their sadness. We have to put in the time without expecting anything in return.

Befriending someone is a powerful act. Spending time with Becky wasn't difficult; in fact, the more I got to know her, the more I realized how much wisdom she was passing on to me. Becky was one of the first women to graduate from UNC Chapel Hill. And while she never married, she lived a rich professional life, traveling across the state in her job with the state health department. Now she liked to sit on her front porch and watch the birds, but she still loved to smile, and if someone was willing to come by for a visit, she loved to share a bit of her accumulated wisdom. Ninety years of experiences, both good and bad. A life well lived.

When Becky died, I didn't feel particularly sad. I knew that I would miss her, but she was ready to leave this earth. She was at peace with death. She had no regrets. When my own days are numbered, I hope I get to leave like that – that's another lesson Becky taught me.

A few months after Becky passed away, I drove by the old white house and was surprised to find that it was gone. Just an empty field of weeds that needed to be cut, the bird feeders nowhere in sight.

"What happened to Miss Becky's house?" Cason said from the back seat.

"I don't know," I replied.

"What's gonna to happen to her birds?" Brett asked.

I shrugged my shoulders as I drove slowly by the empty lot. "I guess they'll have to go somewhere else."

We sat in silence for a while. I thought about all the hours we'd spent in that yard, visiting with Becky. All the times that

Brett and Cason complained about having to go to her house, only to be glad they went each time, their knees caked in dirt and their faces covered with vanilla ice cream. When they grow up, I hope they will have a friend like Becky. Until then, I hope they will remember the way she used to laugh, silently but with her mouth wide open and her eyes closed, her face filled with joy.

How do we serve our friends? And is friendship even a form of service?

I believe that it is. We also have to consider the kind of friends that we make – some friends are easy; others are hard. Some friends make us feel like the best versions of ourselves, while other friends challenge our patience in ways that are incredibly uncomfortable.

My brother Rob has always been my best friend. Growing up, we shared a bedroom together. We love the same sports, the same books. We've taken cross-country road trips together, and we never get tired of each other's company. I know exactly what my brother is thinking, and he can read my mind as well. We've always been there for each other. Rob is an easy friend to have.

My wife is also my best friend – after all, when you decide to spend the rest of your life with someone, you better enjoy that person's company. My friendship with Rob is rooted in the bonds of blood; my friendship with Jenni takes on a different dimension because I have chosen to bind myself to this person who was once a stranger to me. Rob and Jenni represent different kinds of friendship, but I value each of them equally.

Most friendships are not like this. I am an introvert, so making new friends is not always easy for me. I love people, but I love to be alone as well. My wife feeds off of the energy of a crowd, while a social gathering usually leaves me feeling exhausted. I shouldn't expect to have a whole army of friends because true connections require a lot of work. But that doesn't mean I should avoid friendships; I have to learn to trust people.

Most of us know what it feels like to have our trust broken. When I think about my friends, I guess I should include my ex-girlfriends as well. When I found out that one of my college girlfriends had cheated on me, I felt like my world had been ripped apart at the seams. *Why did this happen?* I wondered. *What did I do to deserve this?* For all I know, I didn't do anything wrong. But I still felt like a part of my identity had been stripped away; if I couldn't trust this person anymore, how could I trust anyone? Looking back, I know that sounds overdramatic, but the pain was very real to me then.

My anger has faded over the years, and it has been replaced with the understanding that my girlfriend and I weren't right for each other. What if we had stayed together? I never would have met Jenni, and I don't want to consider what my life would be like without her. My ex-girlfriend has moved on with her life as well. She's living in California, I think. We don't stay in touch, so I don't know for sure. But I am grateful for the time we spent together. The good and the bad always blend together when we think about our past, and we often weigh these two sides against each other. We wonder which side has taught us more – the good moments or the bad moments, even though they are inextricably bound together. We have to embrace the good and the bad. Friendship is like that. We open ourselves up to another person knowing that they are as deeply flawed and imperfect as we are. One of us is bound to hurt the other one at some point. But we still need each other, even in the midst of this brokenness.

In his bestselling book *Bowling Alone: The Collapse and Revival of American Community*, Robert Putnam points out a troubling societal trend: people have become increasingly disengaged from their neighbors, their community, and civic organizations. Putnam argues that technology has "individualized" people's leisure time; the more time we spend alone, the more isolated we get from each other. Friendships help us to feel connected to our community. Not only do they make us happy, but they also set the foundation for our civic engagement. Democracies are built on these bonds, and our society will only be strong if its people are connected to each other.

Bowling Alone was published in 2001, almost six years before the release of the first iPhone. Since then, cell phones have evolved into mini-laptops with the power to connect us to anyone in the world, at any time. And in spite of this, we feel more isolated than ever before. Instead of meeting with our friends face to face, we spend countless hours scrolling through the social media feeds of our online friends – those loose collections of high school acquaintances and friends-of-friends that primarily exist in the digital world. We maintain these distant connections while our real-world friendships suffer. Some experts even argue that social media is responsible for the dramatic decline in teenage pregnancies over the past ten years. If this is true (and that's a big if), it would be a pleasant side effect to what is, on a global scale, a more troubling trend: we would rather sit at home alone on our phones than connect with people in the flesh.

Over the course of my life, I have been a good friend and I have been a bad friend. One of my college roommates, Anthony, went through a horrible divorce in his late twenties. I remember meeting him for dinner soon after the papers were filed. Anthony was a wreck. I could tell he'd been crying, and the only thing he could talk about was all the ways his marriage had fallen apart. So what was I supposed to do? I was happily married, and while I never really cared for Anthony's ex-wife, it broke my heart to see him so unhappy. He was grieving the loss of his life as he knew it. I didn't know what to say; I sat there with him in a near-empty restaurant, staring at my plate of food. Guys aren't supposed to offer a shoulder to cry on. We're supposed to internalize things. Move on. Never let 'em see you sweat. But the best thing I could do for my friend was to be present with him. And I *was* present, at least for an evening.

In the coming months, Anthony and I would get together from time to time, and while he was slowly piecing his life back together, he was still grieving. He was deeply unhappy. Who wants to be around someone who is unhappy? I certainly don't. I have a hard enough time staying happy when things are going well in my own life. But that's no excuse. I was being a coward; I was afraid to bear witness to Anthony's pain.

I still stay in touch with Anthony, but we've become Christmas-card friends. He's busy with his life. I'm busy with mine. I'm ashamed to admit that I stopped being present in his life. Stepping into Anthony's grief made me uncomfortable. Unfortunately, most of us are hard-wired to act this way when life gets hard, avoiding intimacy at all costs. Friendships can make us squirm. They are not always fun. But when your life starts to unravel, a good friend can save you from your own worst impulses.

Being a good friend is an act of bravery, no less than serving meals at a soup kitchen or tutoring at a low-income school. We don't have to be good at it, necessarily, and we don't have to bring anything special to the relationship. We simply have to be open to someone else. We have to really listen to them. We have to open ourselves up again and again, no matter how painful or awkward it may be.

I think about the high school version of myself – the boy with low self-esteem who switched from the tiny private school to the big public high school. I didn't know anything about anything. I was afraid of people who were different from me. I was scared to make new friends because I didn't want someone to reject me or to make fun of me. I get uncomfortable just thinking about these memories.

For much of my adult life, that's how I thought about the teenage version of myself. I was a failure. I was a coward. There is some truth to this; I *was* a mess in high school, but most of us are a mess in high school. For years I've looked at my failures as a fixed part of my past, defining me and setting the parameters for who I've become as an adult. And yet … I wasn't a complete failure back in high school. Like I mentioned earlier, we need to be aware of our failures, but we also need to amplify the times when we become the best version of ourselves.

For me, the best version of myself occurred when I joined a high school football team. I grew up in Gastonia, North Carolina. Like many southern towns, Gastonia has a complicated history with race. A railroad track divides the city in half. White people live on one side, and black people live on the other. Since I went to a small, predominantly white private school, I didn't have to think about this. When I transferred to the local public high school, race hit me head on. I was one of the few white kids on our football team. Most of the black kids lived on the other side of the railroad tracks. If you were a successful black student, you went off to college and rarely came back to Gastonia. This created a brain drain in the black community, with countless people feeling powerless and angry. Those railroad tracks divided my hometown in countless ways; white people didn't understand black people, and black people didn't understand white people.

I was no different from many of the white people in Gastonia. Before transferring to a public school, I rarely had a chance to interact with black people. When you are young and ignorant like I was, you fill in the gaps with whatever makes sense. You make assumptions. Confusion turns to fear, and before you know it, a person with dark skin almost seems like an alien being. You don't even try to understand them because what's the point? Nothing you say or do can erase these misconceptions. This is how racism takes root in a community.

My life would have been a whole lot simpler if I had stayed at that private school. Definitely not better, but simpler.

Where would I be today if I hadn't made the switch? I'd be a very different person, that's for sure.

By my junior year of high school, I was one of the few players on the football team who had a car. It didn't take long for guys to start asking me for rides. At first I said yes because I was afraid to say no. I was afraid of *them*, to be honest. I'm not proud of this. But I am proud of the fact that I said yes, because that yes would eventually redefine the way I look at race.

Every day after practice, four or five of my black teammates would hop in my car, and I would make the 15-minute drive to the north side of town to take them home. I've talked before about the importance of time, about the daily process of sitting next to someone and building their trust. At first my teammates and I would sit in silence, or I'd blare hip-hop music as a way of covering up the awkwardness. I had to do *something* to fill the silence. After all, what did we possibly have in common? What could we possibly say to each other?

Time made that awkwardness go away. In a few weeks I turned the music down and started to ask my teammates questions about their families, their girlfriends, their hopes and dreams, what they wanted to be when they grew up. Their answers weren't all that different from mine. This was a revelation to me. It was probably a revelation to them too. I didn't always say the right things, and I didn't always listen well to what they said to me – after all, race is a complicated beast that weaves its way into the fabric of our lives, defining not only our past but our future. But every day, when they asked me for a ride home, I said yes.

I learned that Jamie's father had walked out on his family when Jamie was a little boy. Football was his way of calling out to his dad, hoping that one day his dad would be proud of him, maybe come to one of his games and watch with pride as he carried our team on his broad shoulders. Then there was Nick, who was soft-spoken and deeply intelligent. He wanted to join the Marines, see the world, then come back to Gastonia and help the next generation of kids growing up. He had a soft spot for young people, and he wanted to open his own day-care. John was the comedian on our team, and he could always make us laugh with his spot-on impersonations of our teachers, coaches, and fellow teammates. He could impersonate anybody, which, now that I look back on it, was really his way of showing us that he closely observed everyone. In another life he could have been an anthropologist or a sociologist. Instead, he was stuck in a mill home with a leaky roof and too many bills to pay. Yet he still found a way to make us laugh.

My teammates became my friends. I entrusted them with my own backstory so that I could appear human to them as well. We showed up for each other day after day, and sometimes that's all it takes for a true connection to occur.

We live in a divided America. Democrats and Republicans don't talk to each other. Slogans like "Black Lives Matter" have been weaponized in the ongoing battles over race and inequality. Trolls manipulate social media. Religious denominations split into factions over issues like gender and immigration. We go bowling alone and scroll through digital feeds instead of talking to someone face to face. We don't listen to each other's stories anymore.

But it doesn't have to be this way. We need to fight against the tide of our broken culture. We need to stand up for those who are marginalized and voiceless. We need to seek out new friendships and rekindle old ones. This will take courage. This will take vulnerability.

These days I continue to say yes in my role as a teacher, a neighbor, and a friend. I try to keep my heart open and to listen to what people have to say. To *really* listen. What would this world be like if we did more listening instead of clamoring to make our voices heard? Some of our enemies would turn into friends – not all of them, perhaps, but some of them. And that's what it will take to bind our communities back together.

Family

I'm saving family for last.

What good does it do to serve the people outside of our homes if we don't serve the people within?

I am a parent, a spouse, a sibling, and a son. Most of us fit into one of these categories, although far too many of us come from broken homes where none of these labels fit. This is one of the greatest tragedies of all. When I look at my two boys sleeping soundly at night, I wonder how any father could abandon his children. I would take a bullet for my sons. I would do anything to help them grow into men of character. And if, God forbid, they were to die before me, I would have a hard time finding a reason to carry on. When I think about parents who have lost a child, I think about bravery in its purest form. How do parents find a reason to live when a child has been taken from them? But death happens, and these parents continue to live, pouring their hearts into causes that bring meaning to their own lives and honor to their lost child. In this case, service is getting up in the morning and showing people that you are a survivor. You will carry on. You will bear witness to the sanctity of life by carrying on in spite of everything.

I have never stopped loving my children. They mean the world to me. But when I was coaching football for hours on end, or when I was pursuing fame and attention through my work, I sometimes allowed myself to think that being a good father wasn't enough. I had to make a difference in the world. Changing diapers wasn't enough. Reading bedtime stories wasn't enough. Being present with my children wasn't enough. I needed to serve the world in some larger capacity. Otherwise, could I really consider my life a success? These thoughts crept up on me slowly over time. I don't think that I've ever been a neglectful father, but I could have been a more present father. These days I'm trying to make up for lost time.

When our second son Cason was born, Jenni and I decided that she would stay home for a few years to take care of the boys. When we looked at her salary and subtracted the cost of putting two kids in full-time daycare, we realized that we would have about $100 left over each month. That's $100 so that my wife could drive 45 minutes to work and let someone else raise our children. I understand why people do this. I understand what gets sacrificed when you take time off of work, how a professional life can feed our creativity and our need to stay connected to the larger world. But after watching Jenni make this sacrifice for our family, I can honestly say that she has demonstrated the most important form of service in the world.

Raising a child is hard. Raising two children under the age of three is even harder. I remember leaving for work one morning when Cason was a tiny baby and Brett was a toddler. Cason was latched to Jenni's chest and Brett was hanging around her neck.

"Have a great day," I said as I kissed Jenni goodbye.

"How?" she said with a look of complete exhaustion on her face.

I waved awkwardly as I slowly backed out of the house.

Those early days were incredibly hard for Jenni, but she handled them with an enormous sense of calm. She loves to be with our boys, and when she plays with them, they are the center of her world. Think about what that does for a child, waking up each day and knowing that you are loved unconditionally. Jenni makes me want to be a better father and a better husband. What if I looked at her that way when she talked to me, as if nothing mattered in the world but the two of us in that moment as we faced each other? It would make her feel deeply loved, and she would carry that feeling over to our kids, loving them all the more freely, the cycle repeating itself again and again for years to come.

Every one of my professional accomplishments will mean nothing if I can't be a good husband to Jenni and a good father to Brett and Cason. This is the ultimate form of service. They are counting on me, and I can't let them down.

I see brokenness all around me. My friend Anthony grieves at the end of his marriage. My teammate Jamie wishes his father had not walked out on him. My students struggle to deal with a parent's substance abuse. But when I ask my students if they want to get married and have a family when they grow up, almost all of them say yes. In spite of all evidence to the contrary, they want to be a good husband. They want to be a good mother. They know that family is important, and that serving our family is one of the most sacred things we can do on this earth.

Serving our family is also a never-ending cycle. When our children grow up, we become parents to our own mothers and fathers. I'm starting to see this with my parents. My dad recently turned 70, and his body is already starting to fail him. He walks with a cane. He gets tired easily. His mind is still as sharp as ever, but he can no longer provide for his family like he used to. For the most part, he's handling this with grace. He's at peace with death, neither fearing it nor thinking too much about it. Of course, this drives my mom crazy sometimes. She's in better shape than my dad, but she's slowing down as well. I look at my parents and forget, sometimes, that they once created a shield of protection around me. They healed my childhood wounds and gave me advice when I needed it. They put a roof over my head and kept me well-fed. This freed me up to dream big and to tackle any challenge that came my way. Now I am tending to their wounds, giving them advice, providing a roof over my mom's head when my dad gets airlifted to Duke Hospital, listening to their hopes and fears and providing a safety net for them – my parents who are moving closer and closer to their final days.

At first it was hard to watch my parents grow old. I still wanted to see them as my protectors, even though I didn't need their protection anymore. They gave me this gift – for decades they made sacrifices and taught me how to grow up so that I could be a good parent one day. Every milestone fills them with pride, making all of their sacrifices worthwhile.

So now I watch my parents get older and grapple with their own burdens. They are a monument to life, to courage, to persistence – surviving cancer, overcoming grief, continuing to laugh in spite of their many obstacles and disappointments. Now I have a chance to repay them for their sacrifices, protecting them in their final years and bringing them joy as they watch their grandsons thrive, creating a new generation of Albrights, the cycle repeating itself again and again.

Death comes to all of us eventually. Maybe I'll live to be 90 like my friend Becky. I'm not sure I want to stick around that long unless Jenni is still alive too. I know that I don't want to be a burden to Brett and Cason. That's part of service too. As long as I am alive, I want to contribute in some meaningful way. I want to do right by my body, exercising and eating well so that perhaps I can live longer and spend less time in the hospital when I get older. Or I could do everything right and still die tomorrow. We are only promised today. So if that's the case I shouldn't worry about the future, about the things that are out of my control. I should live every day as if it is my last, honoring the life that has been given to me by loving my family, serving others, and focusing less on myself. Then, if I'm lucky enough to stay alive for a few more decades, perhaps I can say that I have honored the life that was given to me.

I wonder what my final years will be like. The world will move on without me. I'll sit on porches contemplating the past, watching the present pass by in the form of school buses and mothers jogging by on their morning run. I should have asked Becky about this before she died. When did life start to slow down for her? Did it ever lose its meaning? I hope not. I don't think it did, because her eyes were always sparkling and she never stopped laughing.

If I live to be 90 years old, I want to keep laughing too.

I've come to the end of this book, and I don't know whether to feel happy or sad. Writing about service has given me some clarity. I see where I am making a positive impact on the world, and I see where I need to do better. I hope that's a step in the right direction.

My sadness stems from the fact that this journey is coming to an end. I love a slow-burning adventure, whether it's writing a book, or taking a road trip with my brother to Alaska, or reading the Harry Potter series with my sons. I like a journey because it forces my eyes to stay fixed on the horizon. I want to serve my wife and my sons and my neighbors and my students. I want to keep my eyes facing forward, never backward.

If we look forward, we will see beauty all around us. But if we fold inward, we will be blind to the many things that make life worth living. We will miss the afternoon sun as it shines through a tree in autumn, the orange and yellow leaves sparkling like fireworks in the sky. We will miss the chance to help someone in need, or to learn something new about a friend – something that never would have been obvious just by looking at them. If our eyes are open to the beauty all around us, we will rejoice in good health after a long illness, never taking our health for granted again. We will slow down and be present with the people we care about, treasuring ordinary time and being content with life in its present form.

We will realize that while we are small, our world is full of opportunities to love others and to live a life of service.

As members of the human race, we have a responsibility to look after those who are less fortunate than we are. All of us will need help at some point in our lives. As long as we have a beating heart, an open mind, and eyes to see the needs around us, there will always be more work to do.

Service is the best possible work. And when we are in the thick of it, service becomes something greater than work. Service brings light out of darkness and gives life to those who no longer feel like getting up in the morning.

My son Cason said it best: *This is the good thing.*

Yes, this is the good thing indeed.

Acknowledgements

I am grateful to have so many wonderful people in my life. My co-workers inspire me, my friends lift me up, and my family loves me more than I deserve. I want to send a special thank you to my parents, Nancy and Alan Albright, my brother Rob and his wife Molly, and the wonderful family I have married into: Joe and Lil Summerville, along with Will and Ali Summerville.

I am incredibly blessed to be married to Jenni Albright. You have always picked me up when I am down, and this book would not exist without your love and your support.

Thank you, Brett and Cason, for bringing so much joy into my life. You inspire me to be a better father and a better man.

Finally, this book is dedicated to LaDwaun Harrison, a friend and fellow coach for over 17 years. This book came out of a difficult time in my professional life, and you stood by me through all of it. Thank you.

About the Author

Stuart Albright is the recipient of the Milken National Educator Award (dubbed the "Oscars of Teaching" by *Teacher Magazine*.) In 2006, he was named the Durham Public Schools Teacher of the Year. Albright holds a B.A. in English and Creative Writing from UNC Chapel Hill and an M.Ed. from Harvard University. He is the founder of McKinnon Press, a company that promotes literacy through the publishing of student work. He is also a freelance editor and lecturer on issues of urban education. Albright can be reached at www.stuartalbright.com.